...ons
of a
boy-crazy
girl

ON HER JOURNEY FROM
NEEDINESS TO FREEDOM

paula hendricks

MOODY PUBLISHERS

CHICAGO

All Scripture quotations, unless otherwise indicated, are taken from the ESV® Bible (*The Holy Bible, English Standard Version*®), copyright © 2001 by Crossway. 2011 Text Edition.

Scripture references marked NIV are taken from the Holy Bible, New International Version®, NIV®. Copyright © 1973, 1978, 1984 by Biblica, Inc.™ Used by permission. All rights reserved worldwide. www.zondervan.com. the "NIV" and "New International Version" are trademarks registered in the United States Patent and Trademark Office by Biblica, Inc.™

All emphases in Scripture quotations have been added by the author.

Edited by Lydia Brownback
Interior design: Erik M. Peterson
Cover design: Kathryn Duckett
Cover image: © Alberto Bogo (iStock 5/10/2010)
Author photo: Katie Bollinger (Photography by Katie)

Library of Congress Cataloging-in-Publication Data

Hendricks, Paula, 1983-
  Confessions of a boy-crazy girl : on her journey from neediness to freedom / Paula Hendricks.
     pages cm
  Includes bibliographical references.
  ISBN 978-0-8024-0750-4
  1. Teenage girls—Religious life. 2. Christian teenagers—Religious life. 3. Trust in God—Christianity. 4. Teenage boys. 5. Interpersonal relations in adolescence I. Title.
  BV4551.3.H46 2013
  248.8'33—dc23

                                                         2013021074

We hope you enjoy this book from Moody Publishers. Our goal is to provide high-quality, thought-provoking books and products that connect truth to your real needs and challenges. For more information on other books and products written and produced from a biblical perspective, go to www.moodypublishers.com or write to:

Moody Publishers
820 N. LaSalle Boulevard
Chicago, IL 60610

3 5 7 9 10 8 6 4

Printed in the United States of America

Praise for *Confessions of a Boy-Crazy Girl*

Teenage girls often look to others for security and significance—most often, it's boys. Good-looking boys. That was me at the age of sixteen, and had someone put this book in my hands back then, who knows the heartaches I could've avoided. *Confessions of a Boy-Crazy Girl* is a must-read for today's young women!

> —**JONI EARECKSON TADA**, CEO/Joni and Friends
> International Disability Center

What a joy it has been to watch Paula on her "journey from neediness to freedom." The transformation has been nothing short of remarkable. Her reflections on that journey are honest, engaging, refreshing, and insightful. In this book, young women will find Paula to be a relatable, caring, wise friend. She will make you laugh; she will make you cry; she will make you think. And she will point you to the only true Satisfaction for a heart that longs to be chosen and cherished.

> —**NANCY LEIGH DEMOS**s, author, *Revive Our Hearts*
> radio host

Love the boy. Hate the boy. Long for the boy. Wait for the boy. If you want off the roller coaster ride of romance, this book is your ticket. In a style that feels like a great conversation with a good friend, Paula gives us front row seats to her up-and-down ride on the roller coaster of love and then teaches us that there is a better way. You will be encouraged, inspired, and entertained by her story, and ultimately you'll find the surprising secret to the lasting Love you're looking for.

> —**ERIN DAVIS**, author of the One Girl series

There are not many words that describe this book . . . because it was amazing. I cannot tell you how much it related to me and gave me the example and Scripture I needed to get through my obstacles. I am *really* boy crazy and love the thought of love, but this book helped me in more ways than could be counted.

> —**GINNI MATHIS**, a teen reader

With encouraging transparency, deep faith, and wisdom learned in the crucible of pain, Paula Hendricks invites us into her heart. As I read, I saw myself over and over again: as a "boy-crazy girl" and as a woman who has been taught by Christ that He "is in the business of transforming broken girls into beautiful trophies of His grace." Nothing is more soul-satisfying than the realization that surrender of all to Him is not a loss at all. If you are a boy-crazy girl (or woman) or if you're a mom or grandmother who knows one, this book is a wonderful resource. I heartily recommend it!

—**ELYSE M. FITZPATRICK**, author of *Found in Him:*
The Joy of the Incarnation and Our Union with Christ

Here is warm, wise, and clear-headed counsel from someone who has dug past the surface and has identified the root cause of boy-craziness. Paula knows firsthand about the "expulsive power of a new affection." Take the quiz in the first chapter and see if this book is for you or for someone you know.

—**BOB LEPINE**, cohost, *FamilyLife Today*

Paula allows us to take a peek into her life through stories, transparent journal entries, and God's guidance along the way. She's relatable, humorous, practical, and just plain real. Gospel-saturated and biblically sound, *Confessions of a Boy-Crazy Girl* provides wisdom for young girls, teens, and moms navigating the tendencies of our boy crazy hearts. Paula has written a book that gives hope for every boy crazy girl.

—**TRILLIA NEWBELL**, author, *United: Captured by God's*
Vision for Diversity

Paula Hendricks has charged right into the heads and hearts of most females with her *Confessions.* I wish I could've read this book as a young teen; it addresses so many common temptations and provides gospel-centered help. With refreshing transparency, Paula invites the reader into her struggles with image, beauty, insecurity, lust, and of course—

guys! Paula comes alongside the reader as a friend and opens her heart to tell her story. She doesn't run from the tough questions, but uses Scripture to grapple with the heart issues. If you're a teen, you need this book. If you're a parent or you have input into young women's lives, you need this book. May the life lessons Paula shares here impact the next generation for God's glory!

—**KIMBERLY WAGNER,** True Woman blogger and
author of *Fierce Women: The Power of a Soft Warrior*

Boy-crazy? It doesn't have to define you! There's a way to get your heart back. Jump inside *Confessions*, get to know Paula, and find your way out. And in the process, you'll discover that the true love you seek is actually seeking you.

—**CARRIE WARD**, author, *Together: Growing Appetites for God*

A great read that is both poignant and relevant to teens today. Paula speaks truth into the lives of her readers in a way that convicts, motivates, and inspires. I know it inspired me!

—**KATIE**, a teen girl

Confessions of a Boy-Crazy Girl is so brutally honest and biblically encouraging that I wish I had read it when I was younger. Like Paula, I also believed that all I had to do was trust God enough and be pretty enough to attract a boy. *Wrong!* If you're the least bit boy-crazy like Paula (and like me) you will be thoroughly encouraged challenged in your faith and relationships.

—**RENEE FISHER**, the Devotional Diva, is an author of four books including *Not Another Dating Book* and *Loves Me Not*. She writes for young adults at http://www.devotionaldiva.com

In *Confessions of a Boy-Crazy Girl,* Paula bravely opens her heart and journals to confess what many young women struggle with—a deep need for a guy's approval. This raw and honest look into her journey will encourage others to seek the One worthy of seeking. Paula shares how God helped her step off the crazy cycle of heartbreak over meaningless crushes and get on to a more meaningful relationship with Him.

> —**HEATHER PATENAUDE**, author of *Emotional Purity: An Affair of the Heart*

I've watched dozens of "boy-crazy girls" wrestle with God on their journey of trying to find love, value, and acceptance in romantic relationships. In *Confessions of a Boy-Crazy Girl,* Paula intentionally reorients *all* girls to the gospel with gut-level openness and honesty, and for that I am grateful.

> —**BRAD NEESE**, student ministry pastor (and daddy of two beautiful girls)

Confessions of a Boy-Crazy Girl takes an honest look at the core heart issues that hide behind the lies and mind games that can keep you trapped in the repeat cycle. Sprinkled with humor and filled with biblical truth and realistic wisdom it navigates you on your own heart-searching truth journey pointing to a new direction, purpose, and resolution. In the end, it will encourage you to believe unashamedly with Paula and others, "This was me before Christ transformed me from the inside out. This is the radically different person I am today—crazy after Christ!"

> —**SUSAN HENSON**, founder of Pure in Heart Conference Ministries, coauthor of *Life Lessons from the Princess and the Kiss* and *Life Lessons from the Squire and the Scroll*

To my parents, John and April Hendricks,
for instilling a God-consciousness in me from birth.
And for keeping such close tabs on me
during those tumultuous teen years!
At the time, I thought you were just plain ol' mean,
but now I can't thank you enough for sparing me a harvest of regret.
Thanks for forgetting all about those days of rebellion.
Today I count you the dearest of friends
and am so grateful for your love and support.
I love you!

Contents

Foreword

I wish you could meet her.

Really spend time with her and look into her eyes. See the snow white of her skin and the cascade in her brunette hair.

It's not just on the surface. It's something deeper. The sparkle in her eyes. The purity under the surface of her skin. The gentleness that bursts from within holds her gentle waves as a mere complement.

Paula Hendricks is a true beauty.

That made it a little hard for me to read the raw confessions of self-loathing in these pages. Made it hard for me to understand how her eyes could not see her beauty. And thought the presence of a guy would be the evidence of it.

But that is the beauty of this book.

Paula is transparent about her struggle to find contentment in God's plan for love.

Which of us has not struggled to see our beauty?

To accept God's plan for romance?

Believing that we need a guy to complete us is one of the most prevalent lies young women tend to believe. When I had the honor of working with Nancy Leigh DeMoss to write *Lies Young Women Believe*, we conducted focus groups across the nation. We asked teen girls if they believed the statement, "I would feel better about my life if I had a boyfriend." Sixty-eight percent strongly agreed.

Think about that.

Your life would be better with a guy?

You're *that* needy?

Paula hits the nail on the head when she writes: "Boy craziness is really just girl neediness."

What do you *need*?

I'm not going to tell you here, because the pages of this book do it so very well. Like a great novelist, Paula will take you through the ups and downs of her love life until you find the thrilling (but not so conclusive) conclusion. Yep, this one's gonna be a cliff-hanger, but that cliff is the place where you jump off into freedom.

And, oh, how I want to see you get free from the counterfeits we stuff into our needy hearts as girls. Boys. Beauty. These are two of the most difficult to navigate topics for the female heart, and yet they are so important. We cannot deny ourselves the struggle.

You see, marriage as God designed it is a picture of our romance with Him. You would never consider painting a picture of something without first looking at the Original, right? But that is what we do when we try to stuff beauty and boys into our neediness without first looking into the eyes of Jesus for what we need.

In the pages of this book, Paula will use her story and the Word of God to transform your mind. You'll turn from being a "beauty grasper" into a "beauty gazer" and from a boy-crazy needy girl into a God-satisfied woman of freedom.

Praying over this book and your heart today as I write this.
Dannah Gresh
Bestselling author, *And the Bride Wore White* and *Get Lost: Your Guide To Finding True Love*

before
we dive in

This book (and my story) recently took a surprising turn. It looked like it was shaping up to go something like this: *Trust God with your love life, and when you do, watch Him deliver the gift you've always wanted—wrapped up beautifully with a nice, neat bow.*

Now though, once again, things haven't turned out like I thought they would—and this story is quite different (and more realistic, I think). *Trust God with your love life, and buckle up for the ride!*

While I never would have said this, in reality I was treating God like a math equation: *this* plus *this* plus *this* equals *that*. In my case, it was: trust God + wait on God + pray about everything + be led by Scripture = getting the guy and the love I've always wanted.

But I never was any good at math. And God is not a formula.

God is a Person—one who's more interested in securing my *forever* happiness than my *temporary* happiness. Hard to believe, but as my Creator, He knows better than I do what will truly make me happy. And, ultimately, the ache I'm looking to fill will never be satisfied by anyone or anything other than Him.

But how can an invisible God satisfy when all I want is a pair of strong arms to hold me close?

That's what I hope to answer through this book as I share my journey with you—the good, the bad, and the ugly. It's a story of high hopes dashed by disappointment and pain, followed by more hope, disappointment, and pain. But it's also a love story— the story of a sweet, patient, pursuing Love. I believe all the pain I experienced in relation to guys is what God used to drive me to Him—the one I really wanted all along, even though it took me years to realize it.

My prayer is that your pain and disappointment would drive you to Him as well, that you would surrender control and trust God with your love life, and that, as you wait on Him, you would get your deepest needs met in Him. After all, He's the one you've been longing for all along—even if you don't yet see it.

While I hope to point you to the One who alone can satisfy you, my relationship with God won't get you anywhere. It's time to develop a relationship with Him yourself—getting to know Him the way you would any new friend. I hope to help with that, too. Thankfully, He's gone to great lengths to make a relationship with you possible.

Enough prefacing. Let's dive into this journey from neediness to freedom!

Your big sis in Christ,

paula

BoyCrazyGirlBook.com

PART 1

The
SEARCHING
(Doing It My Way)

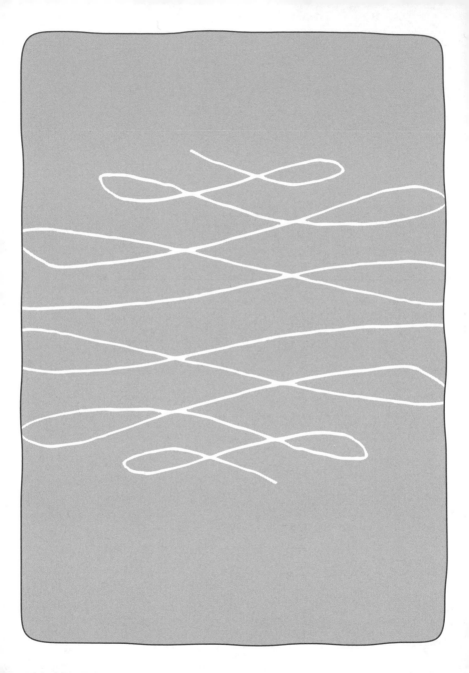

the prayer that rocked my world

It was a desperate prayer I prayed that fall—that God would free me from my idols and teach me to trust Him with my love life. I don't know what I expected, but it certainly wasn't a punch to my gut that left me reeling with shock and my whole world spinning out of control. To say I didn't see it coming would be the understatement of the year. Had I known how God would answer my prayer, I'm not sure I would have had the courage to pray it.

While the light fixtures swung, the walls did the tango, and the evidence mocked, "Your God has purposefully been cruel to you," deep down I knew the truth. This blow was a severe mercy.[1] Yes, it hurt—hurt so bad my tears didn't dry up for months—but I also knew God was answering my prayer in a way that would ultimately bring healing and freedom.

But I'm getting ahead of myself.

I Want Off!

The reason I prayed this bold prayer was that I wanted off my merry-go-round ride that never stopped its perpetual spinning. It went something like this:

1. Spot a cute boy (we'll call him Boy A).
2. Dream about Boy A.
3. Do whatever it takes to make Boy A notice me.
4. Even though Boy A doesn't pursue me, hang on to my dream of Boy A until he (a) moves to the North Pole with no access to a cell phone or computer, (b) dies and is buried or cremated, or (c) begins dating another girl.
5. Mend my broken heart by hating Boy A and finding another cute boy (Boy B).
6. Replace Boy A with Boy B.
7. Dream about Boy B.
8. Make sure Boy B notices me.
9. Hang on to my dream of Boy B until he . . .
10. Move on to another cute boy—Boy C.

The truth is, I went through an entire alphabet—and more—of boys over the years.

Early Beginnings

I was ten years old when I first wrote about a boy in my journal. It didn't seem to matter that his last name was Roach, or that he came in and out of my life one short afternoon. I wrote, "*Dear*

Diary, today I really got to know *Nick Roach! I really like him! I wouldn't ever tell him that!"

Nick Roach wasn't the first boy I noticed. A couple of years earlier I had lain in bed night after night praying, "God, please let me marry Chadwick Chandler Chadderdon. Please let me marry Chadwick Chandler Chadderdon." (If you like tongue twisters, try that one on for size!) I don't remember much about Chadwick, except that he had blond hair, lived on a farm, and was in my Sunday school class.

As the years passed, my "cute, innocent crushes" became more and more frequent—and more and more costly.

But it didn't look that way at first. In high school, my friends thought I was hilarious because I'd pretend I was in love with the most unpopular guys in school. We nicknamed one guy Jello (because of the way his stomach jiggled), and we sent notes back and forth laughing about how much I liked Jello.

If my friends and I had known where my boy craziness would take me, though, we wouldn't have laughed. I was about to experience Psalm 16:4: "The sorrows of those who run after another god shall multiply."

"Little g" Gods and the "Big G" God

I should explain: I wasn't running after one of those fat, little, golden idols. A friend once described a god, or an idol, to me this way: an idol is something that, without it, you think you'll face a "hell"—your own personal version of torment and pain. But with your idol, you think you'll be saved from that hell. Whatever you think will save you from your "hell" is your idol.

Have you ever thought about what your "hell" and idol are? Most of us have more than one, but my main idol was a boyfriend. I thought it would save me from the hell of not being loved.

An idol, or a "little g" god, is a dangerous thing and will always disappoint us. That's because it's a cheap substitute for the "big G" God, the one we were made by and for. This "big G" God is our Creator and the King of the entire universe. Not a cruel, capricious king, but a kind and just King.

In the beginning everyone and everything was subject to the King. But then one of the King's servants decided *he* wanted to be king. Ever since that day he has been leading a rebellion against the King. You may have heard of this servant. His name is Satan. Whether you know it or not, you are now caught up in this cosmic clash—the King desiring (and deserving) your wholehearted love and submission, and Satan wanting nothing more than for you to rebel against the King.

And most have rebelled against the King. When He sent His Son, Jesus, to earth over two thousand years ago, His people hatefully shouted, "We do not want this man to reign over us. . . . Crucify him, crucify him!" (Luke 19:14; 23:21). So they did. Some, though, said, "Truly this was the Son of God!" (Matthew 27:54). And because He was, death couldn't keep Him down. He rose from the dead and returned to the throne room of heaven.

The King of Kings

In Revelation 19:11–16 we're given a sneak peek of Jesus' soon return to earth to destroy His enemies and set up His kingdom for good. Read about it for yourself:

I saw heaven opened, and behold, a white horse! The one sitting on it is called Faithful and True, and in righteousness he judges and makes war. His eyes are like a flame of fire, and on his head are many diadems [crowns], and he has a name written that no one knows but himself. He is clothed in a robe dipped in blood, and the name by which he is called is The Word of God. And the armies of heaven, arrayed in fine linen, white and pure, were following him on white horses. From his mouth comes a sharp sword with which to strike down the nations, and he will rule them with a rod of iron. He will tread the winepress of the fury of the wrath of God the Almighty. On his robe and on his thigh he has a name written, King of kings and Lord of lords.

Did you catch that? Jesus is the King of kings. It doesn't get any higher than that. Jesus is the greatest. The highest. The bestest. (Sorry, I know that's not a word, but I just had to.) As the King of kings, He deserves our fear, our obedience, our honor, and our celebration.

But instead of loving and worshiping the King of kings, I gave my love, worship, and affection to a "little g" god: boys. You'll get to read all about that in the following chapters. But first, let's talk about you.

Your Turn: Take the Boy-Crazy Quiz

Can you relate? Let's stop for a minute so you can take the Boy-Crazy Quiz and find out how you rate. Simply circle yes or no to answer the following fourteen questions. I'm going to make a quick cup of chai while you're working on it. See you in a few!

1. In a room full of people, do you always know where "he" is? (yes / no)
2. Are boys your number-one favorite topic of conversation with your friends? (yes / no)
3. Do you often dress to catch a guy's attention? (yes / no)
4. Do you replace one crush with another almost as soon as you realize the first relationship is not going anywhere? (yes / no)
5. Have you asked a guy out? (yes / no)
6. Do you have your eye on more than one guy at a time? (yes / no)
7. Do you believe you'd finally be completely happy if you had a boyfriend? (yes / no)
8. Do you change your schedule or plans in order to bump into him? (yes / no)
9. Do you tend to have more guy friends than girlfriends? (yes / no)
10. When you're relaxing with a good book, movie, or song, do you pick those that are filled with ooey-gooey romance? (yes / no)
11. If you journal or pray, are your pages or prayers filled with thoughts and requests about guys? (yes / no)
12. Are you always trying to figure out which guys like you? (yes / no)

13. Would you be willing to get a total makeover for a guy? Not the hair, makeup, and new clothes kind, but the "I'll change who I am at my core if that's what it takes to get you" kind? (yes / no)

14. Anything I've missed? If so, write it here:

_____

If you answered yes to any, several, or all of those questions, then keep reading—this book is for you!

∽⟨҈⟩∾

YOUR JOURNAL CORNER

Is your life more marked by submission to or rebellion against the King of kings? What "little g" god are you living for, and what personal version of "hell" do you hope your idol will save you from?

* Many names and details in this book have been changed to protect the privacy of others.

CHAPTER 2

early lessons in love

When my friend Hannah was in eleventh grade, she noticed that peer pressure was getting tougher. So she told her dad, "I think I'll need more hugs than normal." I love that. I wish I'd moved toward my dad during my teen years rather than shutting myself away in my room.

But I didn't. I didn't feel close to my dad. As the gap between us grew, I looked to guys to fill that gaping love hole inside of me.

Don't get me wrong. I'm not saying it was my dad's fault I was boy crazy. As Nancy Leigh DeMoss says, "The outcome of our lives is not determined by what happens to us but by how we respond to what happens to us."[2]

But my relationship with my dad is an important puzzle piece in my boy-crazy tale—just as your relationship with your dad is in yours. Like it or not, our relationship with God is shaped by our relationship with our dad, and our relationship with both God and our dad shapes our interactions with guys.

Missing God in a God-Saturated Home

Growing up, God was as much a part of my life as food, sleep, work, and play. He was the foundation of our home. We read the Bible as a family morning and evening and worshiped God with other Christians every Sunday and Wednesday.

I don't remember a time when I didn't believe that God was holy, holy, holy and that I was desperately sin sick. My parents still have the many apologies I wrote and drew for them when I'd disobey as a little girl.

Almost every night I asked Jesus to save me from my sins. I knew God's standard is perfection, and it wasn't hard to see I didn't measure up. Somehow, though, I missed the fact that Jesus lived a perfect life on my behalf.

Instead, I set out to earn God's love and approval. But, no matter how hard I tried, I never felt I had it. Oh, I knew the Bible says God loves me, but I sure never felt it. How could He? I couldn't begin to meet His standards.

The Good

As I already mentioned, our first understanding of God is shaped by our relationship with our father. I have a great dad. He worked hard to provide for our family. He spent many evenings playing board games and teaching us how to play a mean game of basketball. He bought us candy (I have a serious sweet tooth!) almost every time we stopped for gas. He even helped me with school projects (my favorite: the time he gave my brother a haircut and helped me make a toupee for my book report *What's the*

Teacher's Toupee Doing in the Fish Tank?). I could go on and on about how great my dad is.

But no parent is perfect. Not even the good ones.

The Not-So-Good

It might have been the time I spilled my milk as a little girl. Dad got upset, and I believed from then on that I couldn't mess up. Ever. Or I'd make him mad. I was always on edge, afraid I might set off his anger.

It didn't help that I was sensitive. I cried when I was happy, cried when I was sad, and cried when I didn't even know why I was crying. My dad often told me to cut it out when my tears flowed. The only way I knew to hide my "weakness" was to maintain distance.

So while everything looked good on the outside, I didn't have a close relationship with Dad—or with God. And because of my perception of my dad, I viewed God as an angry, hard-to-please authority figure. I was afraid of Him.

I came to believe I always had to be strong and could never show any weakness in order to have a relationship with my dad, with God, or with guys. I had to have it all together first. I had to be perfect.

Feeling Unloved

By the time I hit my teen years, my relationship with Dad was especially tumultuous. He didn't trust me (you'll understand why in chapters 4 and 5). On top of that, we just didn't understand each other—or even seem to like each other. We both have strong personalities, and we butted heads. A lot. And since I didn't yet understand the importance of treating Dad respectfully, I sent a whole lot of icy glares his direction when I didn't agree with him.

Also, I've always liked to ask tons of questions and have deep conversations. My dad, on the other hand—like many men— preferred talking about the latest sports scores to talking about relationships. He may have felt I was judging him when I probed into his past and tried to understand what made him tick.

All these differences led me to feel unloved and rejected by Dad. So I turned to guys. But here's the thing it took me years to learn: *boy craziness is really just girl neediness.* Boys will never do the trick; only God can fill those empty, needy places.

Miracles Still Happen

At some point, I began to cry out to God for help. Slowly, as I started to believe and receive God's love for me, He freed me up to love my dad. After all, true love doesn't take—it gives.

As I received God's love, He helped me choose to forgive my dad for not being perfect. He helped me release Dad of my expectations. I began to learn to express respect and love for Dad in ways he'd appreciate rather than waiting for him to express his love in the way I wanted. Like this time I captured in my journal:

> *Last weekend, I traveled four hours with Dad to the Buchanans'. I purposely didn't ask him questions, so I think he's more comfortable and happy with our relationship. And lo and behold, today he called me! He asked all about a trip I had just taken. Then he said "I love you" before he hung up.*

2: early lessons in love

That phone call was just the beginning of many sweet surprises to come:

> *My heart is ready to burst. Dad picked me up from college. We talked the whole two hours home. He talked openly to me. He told me he'd been hurt so he had distanced himself. I'm amazed at how You're working, God.*

What He Wasn't Made to Satisfy

Don't get me wrong. It's not like Dad suddenly had a personality transplant and started craving deep conversations. He didn't. But I learned an important lesson: dads are human, too. They have their own hurts, and people who are hurting often hurt others. Sometimes they don't communicate their love to us in ways we recognize.

And that's okay. Because no guy—dads included—was ever meant to give us the love we crave. Check out this solemn warning (and then promised blessing) in Jeremiah 17:5–8:

> Cursed is the man who trusts in man
>> and makes flesh his strength,
>> whose heart turns away from the Lord.
> He is like a shrub in the desert. . . .
> He shall dwell in the parched places of the wilderness. . . .
>
> Blessed is the man who trusts in the Lord,
>> whose trust is the Lord.

He is like a tree planted by water,
    that sends out its roots by the stream,
and does not fear when heat comes,
for its leaves remain green.

The Gift of Your Dad

Maybe your dad is as close to perfect as they come. Or maybe he left when you were little. Maybe he's an alcoholic. Maybe he's in prison. Maybe he just sits in front of the TV, night after night, barely noticing you.

God knows and He cares. In fact, according to Acts 17:26–27, God determined the exact time and place you would live—including your "dad story"—so you would seek God and find Him, the only one who is love.

This God is the "Father of the fatherless" (Psalm 68:5). He loves you with a "Never Stopping, Never Giving Up, Unbreaking, Always and Forever Love."[3]

As you receive your Father God's love for you, don't underestimate what He can do as you forgive your dad, release him from your expectations, and love him with God's unconditional love.

As a teen, I never would have guessed that someday I would feel loved and treasured by my dad. But I do! While writing this book, I got an email from him saying, "I love you, and I love what you're doing." How cool is that? Nothing—nothing—is impossible with God.

YOUR JOURNAL CORNER

How about you? How has your dad influenced your view of God? Do you relate to God more as a loving Father or as a distant authority figure? Either way, would you thank God right now for your "dad story"? It is God's way of encouaging you to seek after and find the only One who can shower you with the love you long for.

awakening love

I'm convinced I caught the boy-crazy bug in junior high partly because of the books I gobbled up—often three a day when school was out! My parents kept a close eye on what I read, much to my frustration. But I don't think they had a clue how these acceptable "Christian" romance novels were forming this boy-crazy girl.

Hour after hour I lost myself in romantic stories about handsome guys and beautiful girls bumping into each other, overcoming misunderstanding and prejudice, and finally getting together. I learned (wrongly) that if a guy is mean to a girl, it's because he secretly likes her. If he's nice, it's because he likes her. In the end, the (nearly perfect) guy always likes the girl, falls for her, and wins her heart against all odds.

I got so swept up in these stories that I felt as though I were the main character. Each time I closed another book, my pillow would be drenched with tears. Tears because the beautiful story had ended. Tears because of the jarring transition back into less-than-perfect real life.

Warning: Don't Awaken Love Until . . .

One of the books I didn't read during that time was the Song of Solomon. It's a little book tucked into the middle of the Bible that tells the passionate love story of a king and a maiden. Not exactly what you'd expect to find in the Bible, I'm guessing! In fact, tradition has it that during the time when Jesus walked this earth, Jews under thirty were not allowed to read this book unless they were married.

Despite its racy content, I think it might have done me good to read it as a teen. Why? Over and over throughout the book the warning is given, "Do not arouse or awaken love until it so desires" (2:7; 3:5; 8:4 NIV), or until the appropriate time.

Song of Solomon 8:7 explains why: "Many waters cannot quench love; rivers cannot wash it away" (NIV). And as the verse before says, "It burns like blazing fire, like a mighty flame."

Can you imagine a blazing forest fire that several rivers' worth of water cannot extinguish? That would be one intense firestorm. This maiden was experiencing the beauty of love and sex as God designed it. But God knows that if we don't wait to experience true love in the safe context of a God-blessed marriage, we will get severely burned.

Tear It Out and Cut It Off

This isn't the only place in God's Word where we're warned not to awaken love before it's time. In the Sermon on the Mount, Jesus unpacks one of the Ten Commandments in a way that will blow your mind. I see some room on the grass there. Let's sit down and listen. He's talking about it now:

> You have heard that it was said, "You shall not commit adultery." (Matthew 5:27)

By the way, adultery is when a married person breaks their covenant promise and has sex with someone who is not their husband or wife. Okay, I'll stop interrupting Jesus.

> But I say to you that everyone who looks at a woman [or man] with lustful intent has already committed adultery with her [or him] in his [or her] heart. If your right eye causes you to sin, tear it out and throw it away. For it is better that you lose one of your members than that your whole body be thrown into hell. And if your right hand causes you to sin, cut it off and throw it away. For it is better that you lose one of your members than that your whole body go into hell. (Matthew 5:28–30)

Whoa, Jesus. Hold on! That's really extreme. You want me to tear out my eyeball or cut off my hand so I won't sin?

For the record, Jesus isn't promoting self-mutilation. He's saying that even if there's something incredibly valuable to you, if it is causing you to sin, then you should get hard core about removing it from your life.

These Books Have to Go

I didn't get radical about saying goodbye to Christian romance novels until I was about eighteen. By then, I'd figured out that whenever I read them, I'd be tempted to lust, and I'd indulge myself in sinful tendencies. This left me feeling guilty and ashamed. But when I desperately cried out to God for help, although the temptation didn't disappear immediately, He began to give me the desire and power to stop fueling the temptation with these books.

In 1 Corinthians 10:13 we're told, "No temptation has overtaken you that is not common to man. God is faithful, and he will not let you be tempted beyond your ability, but with the temptation he will also provide the way of escape, that you may be able to endure it."

While you and I have to expect temptation, we sure don't have to feed it. When I "took this way of escape" by ditching these books, I found I was beating the temptation for the first time! Not perfectly at first, but more and more as time went on.

What about you? Do you need to get serious about not awakening love in your life? How?

Maybe you can read a Christian romance novel without slipping into unhealthy emotional fantasies. What leads me into sin might not be an issue for you. Maybe you're awakening love by who you follow on Twitter or by plastering your bedroom walls or locker with posters of hot guys with steamy looks. I have a friend who has decided not to watch TV by herself. Me, I try to steer clear of:

- Reading romance novels—even "Christian" ones
- Listening to love songs
- Watching most chick flicks
- Sitting next to a guy in close quarters, especially at a movie theater

- Lingering in a car talking with a guy
- Checking out a guy's Facebook page constantly (otherwise known as stalking)

I'm not saying these things are inherently sinful, just that I stay away from them because they can easily lead me into temptation.

Forty Long Days of Temptation

Okay, so if you stay away from tempting situations, are you still going to struggle with tempting thoughts sometimes? Of course! Look at Jesus. Of all people, you would expect Him to be exempt from temptation, right? I mean, He's full of the Spirit (Luke 4:1). He is—God! And yet He is also fully man. And in Luke 4 Satan bombards Him with temptations.

I like the way Dr. J. Oswald Sanders summarizes these temptations (just a heads-up: Dr. Sanders was born in the early twentieth century, so he talks a bit differently than we do). He says, "In each temptation Satan endeavored to induce Jesus to act in a manner contrary to complete dependence on God."[4]

That first temptation seemed so legit. Jesus hadn't eaten anything for forty days. He must have been famished—literally starving to death! The Devil tempted Him to turn stones into bread (which, by the way, would've been as easy for Jesus as it is for us to turn on the faucet and get water). But, in Sanders's words, Jesus "preferred remaining ravenously hungry to moving out of line with His Father's will. He would await His Father's word and provision."[5]

Really?

This wasn't the only way Satan tempted Jesus to move ahead of His Father. Right after this temptation, Satan showed Jesus all the kingdoms of the world and offered Him authority over them all if Jesus would only worship him.

King Jesus was going to rule the world—eventually. But His rise to power would come in a surprising way. Only after Jesus humbled Himself and died the death of a criminal would God the Father exalt Him to the highest throne. In Sanders's words, Satan was offering Jesus the crown without the cross. To accept Satan's shortcut would've been to reject God's plan to offer salvation to the entire world.

Girl, Don't Face That Temptation Alone

Wow. How is Satan tempting you to take for yourself rather than waiting on your Father's way and timing?

Hebrews 2:18 says, "Because he himself has suffered when tempted, he is able to help those who are being tempted." That's you! All you have to do is ask for His help. Remember, He's been there. And He's already defeated Satan on your behalf. That doesn't mean we'll never be tempted; just that this is why it's so important for us to live in the Spirit minute by minute. More on that in chapter 5.

Unfortunately, as you'll read in the next chapter, I was too wrapped up in what I looked like on the outside to care about what was happening inside.

YOUR JOURNAL CORNER

How have you been awakening love? What are some practical ways you can figuratively "tear out your eye" and "cut off your hand" if it's tempting you to sin? Will you write your radical steps here and share them with your mom or a wise friend?

CHAPTER 4

if i could just be beautiful enough: my ticket to love

I was just a little girl when I realized I wasn't as pretty as the other girls. It all started on the playground the day my classmates taunted, "Paula runs like a duck!" I was born bowlegged, but my crooked legs weren't the only thing working against me.

In second grade, I got the most hideous glasses. They covered half my face and were about as thick as two Krispy Kreme donuts. I longed to lose them, but I was blind as a bat without them.

As if that weren't enough, I dressed differently from the other girls. All I wanted was to fit in, but the modest, knee-length shorts my parents made me wear didn't allow for it. That's why, the summer before eighth grade, I recorded these compliments in my journal:

Uncle Norm said in a few years I'd blossom into a beautiful woman. And Aunt Sheri told me she went into our room to get a pillow and stood watching me sleep for a minute. She said I was so pretty-looking (in other words, without glasses). I hope I can get contacts soon.

I didn't get contacts until ninth grade, which is why I was amazed when I actually got some attention from guys in eighth grade:

Guess what?! Angie asked Mike if he liked me, and he said yes. Then today Mike said, "I know something you don't know about Bob." I begged him to tell me, and he said that Bob and a couple other guys said I wasn't bad-looking. You can't imagine how good that makes me feel, even if they didn't say I'm "fine." I feel ugly next to the girls with short shorts and nice legs.

The Fat, Hairy Lies I Came to Believe on My Eighth-Grade Field Trip

Unfortunately, I let my friends talk me into dating Mike (in direct disobedience to my parents), and the beauty lies deepened the day of my eighth-grade field trip:

Before we left, I put on a pair of shorts Cassie let me borrow that were hardly longer than my underwear. I pulled them on and off four times in the school bathroom, not wanting to disobey Dad and Mom but wanting to wear them. I must admit I looked great. I never understood why my parents didn't want me to wear short shorts, but I do now. Bob looked at my legs on the bus. On the way home I did the second bad thing. Angie told me Mike really wanted to hold my hand but was shy. So I made the first move, and we held hands. I liked it.

Two fat, hairy lies were implanted in me that day—*that beauty was my ticket to love* and that *I had to show off my body to be considered beautiful.*

My All-Out Beauty Pursuit

So I spent my teenage years on an all-out beauty pursuit. I whitened my teeth, highlighted my hair, tanned in a tanning bed, bought new outfits at the mall as often as I got a paycheck, and wore revealing clothes when I could get away with it. I wasn't much different from God's people, Israel:

> Your renown went forth among the nations because of your beauty, for it was perfect through the splendor that I had bestowed on you, declares the Lord God. *But you trusted in your beauty* and played the whore because of your renown. (Ezekiel 16:14–15)

For the record, I didn't become a whore. But I did trust in my beauty. I believed that if I could just be beautiful enough on the outside, I would finally be loved—truly loved—by a guy.

But the harder I tried to be beautiful on the outside, the more insecure I felt on the inside. There were always other girls who seemed more beautiful, who showed off more skin—not to mention the perfect photoshopped women whom I knew guys were looking at in magazines and on TV. (How is a girl supposed to compete with that?)

My First Heartbreak

My insecurity only grew when Mike broke up with me over the phone just one month after we started dating. School was out for the summer, and Mike was afraid he'd cheat on me since he wouldn't see me until school started again.

Just as Mike was finishing breaking up with me, he said those three words I'd dreamed of hearing: "I love you." What I longed for seemed so close and yet so out of reach! Apparently his "love" wasn't strong enough to wait two months. Beauty hadn't delivered the love I wanted.

I was heartbroken. When Dad and Mom asked why I couldn't stop crying, I said it was because I missed my friends. I did. But mostly I missed Mike.

It would be years before I realized the beauty and love I was after cannot be manipulated or bought by a few beauty products but are found in the God-Man, Jesus.

A Most Unusual Love

Here's what gets me most about Jesus' love. He loved and rescued you and me when there was nothing beautiful about us. Check it out for yourself in Romans 5. Circle the words that describe who and what you were when Jesus died for you (hint: there are four):

4: if i could just be beautiful enough

While we were still weak, at the right time Christ died for
the ungodly. For one will scarcely die for a righteous person—though perhaps for a good person one would dare
even to die—but God shows his love for us in that while
we were still sinners, Christ died for us. Since, therefore,
we have now been justified by his blood, much more shall
we be saved by him from the wrath of God. For if while we
were enemies we were reconciled to God by the death of
his Son, much more, now that we are reconciled, shall we
be saved by his life. (vv. 6–10)

Did you catch that? Jesus loved us enough to die for us when
we were weak, ungodly, sinners, and His enemies. He loved me
when I chose to rebel against His command to honor and obey
my parents and listened instead to my friends' foolish advice. Did
I suffer the consequences as a result? You'd better believe it! But
did God ever stop loving me? Not for a second.

With a God like that, you don't have to be a beauty grasper like
I was all those years. You can be a beauty gazer instead:

> One thing have I asked of the Lord,
>   That will I seek after:
> that I may dwell in the house of the Lord
>   all the days of my life,
> *to gaze upon the beauty* of the Lord
>   and to inquire in his temple. (Psalm 27:4)

If your goal is to be the hottest girl around, you'll never be satisfied. And even if you achieve your goal, it will be temporary. Sorry to break the news to you, but everyone—even you—will one day stretch, wrinkle, and sag. Hard to believe, I know.

But if you spend time soaking up the Lord's beauty (who, by the way, made the beautiful beaches, the beautiful flowers, and the beautiful you), you will find what you're looking for. His beauty is perfect, and your enjoyment of Him will satisfy your soul.

What Are You Doing with Your Beauty?

Don't get me wrong—I'm not encouraging you to let your body, hair, and nails go. The way you present yourself can either discredit your God in others' minds or draw them to Him. As long as you're not under- or overvaluing your physical appearance, I believe others will be able to see what God values above all—your heart—and ultimately, His Spirit in you. A question I sometimes ask myself is, *Will saying this or doing this or dressing this way distract guys from Jesus?*

Now here's the really cool thing: as you gaze at Jesus by getting to know Him in the Word of God, you will actually become more and more beautiful. Just as the moon doesn't have any light of its own but reflects the sun's light, you will reflect Jesus' beauty to others as you spend time with Him:

> We all, with unveiled face, beholding the glory of the Lord, are being transformed into the same image from one degree of glory to another. (2 Corinthians 3:18)

4: if i could just be beautiful enough

So how about you? What do you believe is your ticket to love? A perfect body? A bubbly personality? A high GPA? Your athletic ability?

Can I save you some time—and some heartache? These "little g" gods won't deliver the love you're after, but Jesus will. He is the source of the breathtaking beauty and love you and every other person on this planet long for.

Sadly, I didn't get this when I was a teen, so before long, I was on to my second boyfriend. The stakes were higher this time, the heartache deeper. Turns out, instead of love, I'd stumbled across its devastating substitute. More on that in the next chapter.

YOUR JOURNAL CORNER

What do you believe is your ticket to love? How has it been working for you? Are you a beauty gazer or a beauty grasper? How could you focus on becoming more of a beauty gazer?

lusting behind my parents' back

Never, as a freshman, did I think I'd turn the head of a varsity football player. Especially Neil, whose smile melted my insides quicker than ice cream on a sultry summer day. But one day I did turn his head (it might have had something to do with the fact that I was still parading around the halls in my friends' itty-bitty clothes):

> *Guess what?! Andy told me Neil likes me and is thinking about asking me out! Today Neil asked me for a picture and wrote our initials with SweeTarts: NT + PH. I can't believe he likes me. I hope he doesn't ask me out 'cause I'll have to say no. I won't go behind my parents' back.*

And I didn't. That year, anyway. But my resolve began to slip sophomore year:

Guess what happened? Same thing as last year. Neil likes me again. Why am I still drawn to him? He's such a player. Sarah told me he came to school with a hickey. Why does he still tempt me?

Neil and I began dating soon after, and that was the last journal entry I wrote for months. I didn't want to risk my parents' finding out I was going out with Neil. Besides, I didn't think I'd ever forget the tiniest detail of our relationship.

Kiss Me

Our first kiss happened so naturally, as "Kiss Me" by Sixpence None the Richer played on Neil's car stereo and his tinted windows hid us from the world. It wasn't long after that I was making out with him in his bedroom while my parents thought I was safe in school studying. I don't know what made me stop him from going farther, but because I did, he soon broke up with me.

While we were in a relationship, I would sometimes feel guilty that I was disobeying my parents (and God!), that I was dating a guy who didn't love Jesus (2 Corinthians 6:14), and that I wasn't living like God's holy daughter:

> Sexual immorality and all impurity or covetousness must
> not even be named among you, as is proper among saints.
> (Ephesians 5:3)

While I occasionally confessed this as sin to God, I didn't have a clue how to change. I felt powerless, swept along by the strong current of my sin.

Sinner or Saint?

It's entirely possible that I wasn't actually a Christian, or a saint, at this point in my life. Oh, I thought I was. But even if I was, I sure didn't understand who I was in Christ. I thought of myself as a sinner, not as a saint. I mean, I knew the Bible called me a saint, but I sure didn't *feel* like one!

How about you? Do you think of yourself as a sinner or as a saint? For the record, by "saint," I don't mean that you've died and that people now pray to you. I'm using *saint* as the Word of God does to refer to a living person who is holy, perfect, and set apart for God. I think Hebrews 10:14 explains a lot:

> By a single offering [Jesus] *has perfected* for all time those who *are being sanctified.*

If you've put your trust in Him, Jesus has already perfected you (past tense), *and* you are currently being sanctified or perfected (present tense). You're a saint who still struggles with sin. Does that sound like double-talk to you? Let me see if I can explain using an example from creation.

Growing into What You Already Are

Is a sapling a tree? Well yeeeees, but not nearly what it *will* be. It looks more like a puny twig than a tree. It will take *years* to grow into a mature tree. But, yes, it's a tree. Even now. It just has some growing to do. And you, if you have been born again, are perfect in God's eyes. Jesus' bloody sacrifice took care of your sin once and for all:

> When Christ had offered for all time a single sacrifice for sins, he sat down at the right hand of God.... For by a single offering he has perfected for all time those who are being sanctified. (Hebrews 10:12, 14)

Are you what you someday *will* be? Oh, no. But does God see you even now as a perfect saint? You betcha! Just like that sapling will someday reach full maturity, you and I will keep working—striving with all God's energy that He powerfully works in us—to grow up into complete maturity in Christ (Colossians 1:29). To grow into what we already are.

You're a Powerhouse

Now that you know what it means to be a saint, let me tell you another important thing I didn't know when I was your age: you're a powerhouse. Oh, I know you probably don't feel like it, but if you've turned from your sins and put your faith in Jesus, His powerful Spirit—the same one who raised Jesus from the dead—now lives in you. Amazing!

You used to have just one way of living—it was always and only life in the flesh. Life controlled by your natural, sinful desires and drives. Now, though, if Jesus has made you a brand-new person with brand-new desires and power to do right, you can "walk by the Spirit, and you will not gratify the desires of the flesh" (Galatians 5:16). Each day, each moment, you have two choices. You can either:

5: lusting behind my parents' back

1. Operate in the flesh

or

2. Operate in the Spirit

At any given point, only the flesh or the Spirit will be in charge. Just as you can't run backward and forward at the same time, you can't live in the flesh *and* the Spirit. Galatians 5:17 says:

> The desires of the flesh are against the Spirit, and the desires of the Spirit are against the flesh, for these are opposed to each other. . . .

Until God gives you an eternal, sinless body, you are going to experience an ongoing fight between the flesh and the Spirit. You will decide who you allow to gain the upper hand by the choices you make. Which is more evident in your life, the works of the flesh or the fruit of the Spirit? (See Galatians 5:19–23.)

The Works of the Flesh	The Fruit of the Spirit
• Sexual immorality	• Love
• Impurity	• Joy
• Sensuality	• Peace
• Idolatry	• Patience
• Sorcery	• Kindness
• Enmity	• Goodness
• Strife	• Faithfulness
• Jealousy	• Gentleness
• Fits of anger	• Self-control

The Works of the Flesh (continued)

- Rivalries
- Dissensions
- Divisions
- Envy
- Drunkenness
- Orgies
- Things like these

Surfing and Life in the Spirit

During college I spent a summer in Maui, where I learned to surf. Years later I heard a pastor say that life in the Spirit is like surfing. You can learn to center yourself on the board, catch a wave, and ride it to shore. But the one thing you cannot do is create a wave, and you sure can't surf without a wave. Similarly, you and I can't live the Christian life without "catching the wave" of the Spirit. He is our power source.

The question is: Are you positioning yourself in such a way that the power of the Spirit can move you?

You can't hope to be filled by the Spirit if you're grieving the Spirit (Ephesians 4:30). Is there any area of your life where you're directly disobeying His commands?

You also can't expect to be filled by the Spirit if you're full of yourself. Matthew 5:3 says "Blessed are the poor in spirit, for theirs is the kingdom of heaven." Are you relying on yourself, confident of your own abilities? Have you realized you can't do life on your own?

You also can't expect to be filled with the Spirit unless you really want to be. He won't force Himself on you. Do you desire to live under the control of God's Spirit, or do you prefer to live life your way? If you answered "my way," will you confess this to King Jesus and ask Him to help you want to live life His way?

In the meantime, begin by doing what I didn't do and make the conscious decision to choose God's way over your way in whatever challenge you're facing.

YOUR JOURNAL CORNER

Are you a sinner or a saint? How do you know? If you are a saint, how can you position yourself so the power of the Spirit can move you like a wave does a surfer? (These would be great questions to discuss with your dad, mom, or a wise Christian friend.)

the relationship in my head

While my relationship with Neil had been touchy-feely, the next was just the opposite: hands-off and in my head. Imaginary.

Oh, I didn't think so at the time. In fact, I naively believed I would marry Caleb. But one day I glimpsed the truth as I tried explaining the relationship to someone.

"How often do you talk?" she asked.

"Only once or twice a year," I replied.

She paused, then bluntly probed, "This relationship is just in your head, then?"

"Well . . . yes," I realized.

Those two words were difficult to get out. But the moment I said them, I saw that my relationship with Caleb had never been more than a fantasy.

Fantasy Beginnings

I met Caleb when I was fourteen. He lived across the country, but we saw each other at church camps and conferences a couple of times a year.

I was nineteen the night I told God I'd like to marry Caleb. We'd just led worship together—me playing the piano, him playing the drums.

The next day, some friends and I went with Caleb to look at a car he was interested in buying. He seemed so smart, talking to the owner about all kinds of things I had no clue about. That night several of us hung out in a pool, and seeing him without his shirt on sure didn't help matters! I wrote down a few of the reasons I liked him:

> *He laughs and talks to people—he isn't shy like I thought— but he won't ever flirt with girls. I love that. He's strong, yet gentle . . .*

That was the beginning of the relationship in my head.

Collecting Evidence

For the next couple of years, Caleb filled my thoughts, journals, and conversations. I became a detective of sorts, searching for clues that he liked me. Anything would do—a look, a smile, a laugh at one of my jokes. When I found out Caleb and I had been assigned to work together again, I wrote:

I've been placed next to Caleb at every single camp. At Lake Ann we led worship. At Hume Lake we performed a skit. At Rock River we looked up verses. And now this. I don't think it's coincidence; I think You're orchestrating something wonderful, God.

Rather than realizing people were pairing us up, I assumed God was. Unfortunately, this wasn't the last time I made that mistake. (Here's hoping you'll learn from me and not count on a future with your crush until he really has pursued you!) In my excitement, I overlooked the important fact that Caleb hadn't made a single move.

Anticipating Our Futures

My best friend Abby and I spent hours talking and dreaming about our futures with Caleb and Cody (her crush). Soon Abby's whole family knew, and our conversations filled me with hope. My journal included entries like this:

Abby and I sat around the kitchen table with her parents talking about the future—Cody and Caleb. I'm sooo excited about how God will work out the details.

How much wiser it would have been to talk to God about Caleb rather than talk to others. Within four months of these conversations, I learned that Caleb was pursuing another girl.

The news came as a total shock.

Your Turn: Take the "Is It in Your Head?" Quiz

How about you? Are you counting on a relationship that's only in your head? Here's a short true/false quiz to help you find out:

1. I talk about my crush more than I talk to him. (true/false)
2. He's never actually told me he likes me, but I have good reason to believe he does. (true/false)
3. I constantly "collect evidence" to convince myself he likes me—smiles, laughter, words, and looks. (true/false)

If you answered *true* to some or all of these questions, you're in danger of counting on a relationship that's only in your head. So what's a girl to do?

Thinking Brand-New Thoughts

Start with your thoughts. It has been said,

Watch your thoughts, for they become words.
Watch your words, for they become actions.
Watch your actions, for they become habits.
Watch your habits, for they become character.
Watch your character, for it becomes your destiny.[6]

Your thoughts matter—big time. In Romans 12:2 we're told, "Do not be conformed to this world, but be transformed by the renewal of your mind." Your mind was never meant to control you—you were meant to control your mind! As you do, you will be transformed from the inside out.

How can you get the upper hand over your thoughts? The answer is found in 2 Corinthians 10:5, "Take every thought captive to obey Christ." Warning: that's a lot of hard, unending work! But it's worth it, because the alternative isn't pretty. Taking every thought captive to obey Christ means you'll have to constantly monitor every thought to see if it passes the Philippians 4:8 test:

> Whatever is true, whatever is honorable, whatever is just, whatever is pure, whatever is lovely, whatever is commendable, if there is any excellence, if there is anything worthy of praise, think about these things.

If a thought doesn't pass the Philippians 4:8 test, rather than letting that thought captivate you, instantly capture it in your mind and turn it over to King Jesus. Then replace that stray thought with a thought that is true, honorable, just, pure, lovely, commendable, excellent, or praiseworthy.

I don't know about you, but I don't have any of those thoughts on my own. I have to borrow Christ's thoughts by memorizing His Words so I can replace my thoughts with His.

Can I encourage you to do the same? If you're not sure where to begin, why not start by memorizing some of the Bible verses in this book? Buy a spiral-bound, index-card notebook from Wal-Mart and write out the ones you find most helpful. Or store them in your phone. It doesn't matter how you do it as long as you get His words into *you*.

If you're in a relationship with Jesus, you now "have the mind of Christ" (1 Corinthians 2:16). Obviously that doesn't mean you're omniscient, that you know every single thing there is to know as God does. But it does mean your mind, which used to be hostile toward Him, can now understand, accept, and think on the things of God. Incredible!

Sneaking Sideways Glances

While we're talking about the importance of our thoughts, we need to talk about our eyes, because there's an important connection. And to talk about our eyes, let's start by getting your mouth watering.

Have you ever tasted Garrett's lip-smacking caramel popcorn? When I lived near Garrett's in Chicago, even the hour-long line couldn't keep me away. Not only was the popcorn finger-licking good; the walls of the shop were covered with mirrors. While I was waiting, I enjoyed sneaking sideways glances at myself.

I have a preoccupation with mirrors. Well, it's deeper than that. I have an eye problem that's connected to a heart problem that's connected to a head problem. I often catch myself glancing sideways to collect evidence—to see what I look like and which guys are watching me. And where my eyes go, my thoughts (and heart) soon follow.

So nearly every morning I pray Proverbs 4:25 and try to do it all day long: "Let your eyes look directly forward, and your gaze be straight before you."

When my eyes are focused forward rather than glancing sideways, my thoughts can't collect the "evidence" they need to convince me of imaginary relationships. Besides, what does it matter if that guy across the street notices me? People and mirrors don't determine my worth.

The Creator of this entire universe thought of me, chose me to be in a relationship with Him through His Son, Jesus. He did this before He poured the foundation of the world and started the clock of time (Ephesians 1:4). If that's not enough to steady my sideways glances and fix my gaze straight ahead, I don't know what is.

How about you? Do you find yourself glancing sideways? Will you join me in asking God to help you look straight ahead the next time you're at the mall, church, or school?

I pray God takes your beautiful face in His hands, reminds you of His love for you, and helps you fix your gaze straight ahead. Because there's nothing imaginary about His crazy love for you—it's so much better than just an imaginary relationship in your head.

P.S. Caleb ended up marrying that girl he pursued. Today they have three kids. Oh, and Abby didn't end up with Cody. She married another guy from camp. They have two kids. And me, well, you'll just have to keep reading to learn what happened to me.

YOUR JOURNAL CORNER

After taking the quiz, do you think it's possible that you're counting on a relationship that's only in your head? How so? Which Bible verse can you start to memorize now so you can start controlling your mind rather than letting your mind control you? Will you write it out here?

forcing a fairy tale

If a guy likes you, he will pursue you." I used to get mad at Mom when she said that, probably because the guys I liked never seemed to like me back. What modern-day girl wants to sit around waiting for her prince to ride into her part of the forest, scale the castle wall, and find her?

With no prince in sight during my college years, I decided to take matters into my own hands and climb out the castle window in search of him. I wrote:

I believe at the core of my being that it's up to me to:
   1) Locate him
   2) Study him
   3) Choose him
   4) Woo him
   5) Perform well enough so he'll ask me to marry him
   6) Marry him
   7) Control him in marriage so he doesn't annoy me too much

I'm not kidding. I actually wrote—and believed—that.

Steps one and two (locate him and study him) were easy enough. I used to spot about fifteen good possibilities a day.

The third step (choose him) wasn't hard either. I could pick a guy lickety-split. Only my choices sometimes got me into trouble:

> *I noticed a cute, intriguing guy when I was boarding the plane. As I approached seat 32B, I realized I would be sitting by him. I "fell" quickly as we talked (I even found out he was a Christian). But about halfway through the flight, I saw a flash of gold on his left hand. I'd been encouraging a married man! I quickly withdrew and picked up the pieces of my heart strewn around my seat.*

After that, I wised up and started looking for a wedding ring before flirting. I was missing the whole point, though. God never intended for me to be constantly on the prowl for a man. Happiness doesn't come from flirting with or securing a guy. Matthew 5:6 tells us we'll experience true happiness when we hunger and thirst not after guys but after righteousness. Matthew 5:8 says the pure in heart are the most happy. They're the ones who will see God—the one we were made for. But I didn't get that, so I kept up the hunt.

Coming Up Short

The fourth step (woo him) was where I always got stuck.

I tried it all. Like Anne of Green Gables, who precariously walked the ridgepole of a house for attention, I once jumped from a banister down a flight of stairs—and promptly twisted my ankle.

Another time I swallowed a live goldfish at the encouragement of some college guys (gross!).

I wasn't always so extreme. Most of the time, instead of being myself I tried to guess at what kind of girl a guy would like. I wrote:

> *If a guy is introverted, I assume he thinks I'm a silly, out-of-control girl. If he's confident and loud, I just know he thinks I'm boring.*

So I faked happy smiles and loud laughter. I left clever gifts and notes for guy friends. And on and on and on. You would think after all that work I'd have ended up on the arm of a prince, but I experienced only disappointment, insecurity, and jealousy.

Who's the Fairest of Them All?

Since my fairy tale was a royal mess, I finally concluded that other girls were my obstacle. Like the queen in *Snow White*, I wanted to be "the fairest of them all." Titus 3:3 described me well: "Passing [my] days in malice and envy, hated by others and hating one another."

I wouldn't have called it jealousy—more like insecurity—but either way it was an awful way to live. In one journal entry I confessed:

> *I hate insecurity more than anything else. It distances me from others. But with so many beautiful, godly, sweet, fun girls, I can never win.*

Anatomy 101

What I didn't understand then was that I was an invaluable member of Christ's body. So was that beautiful girl next to me. And the fun girl next to her. I needed them, and they needed me.

That's the point of Paul's basic anatomy lesson in 1 Corinthians 12. It goes something like this: a body has lots of parts, but it's still one body. That's how it is with you and Jesus if you belong to Him. You're one now. Nothing can separate you. Jesus is the head (the control center), and you are a part of His body. You might be a foot, a hand, an ear, an eye, a liver, or a kidney. Whatever you are, you're vital to the health of the whole body.

See if you can tell from verses 16–25 how this anatomy lesson would have done jealous ole me good (and don't miss Paul's sense of humor):

> If the ear should say, "Because I am not an eye, I do not belong to the body," that would not make it any less a part of the body. If the whole body were an eye, where would be the sense of hearing? If the whole body were an ear, where would be the sense of smell? But as it is, God arranged the members in the body, each one of them, as he chose. If all were a single member, where would the body be? As it is, there are many parts, yet one body. . . . God has so composed the body . . . that there may be no division in the body, but that the members should have the same care for one another.

Can you imagine a body that's just one giant ear? Or a body made up of only one eyeball? That might make for a hilarious picture, but it would be a pathetic body.

You're not any more important than any other part, and yet you're the only one who will ever be able to make much of God with your unique personality, gifts, and even looks. These are all tools you get to use to worship Him and strengthen His body. That's revolutionary.

Those girls you and I are jealous of? If they're Christians, we're a part of the same body. We're on the same team. And even if they're not Christians, they're still handcrafted by God in His image, and He loves them deeply. Thank God for those girls instead of competing with them.

Orphan-Girl Mentality

I know I'm not the only girl who has tried to force a fairy tale. When my seventh-grade friend was asked how her week was going, she wrote,

> *Terrible and more terrible. Long story short, I asked a guy out and he said no and then went out with the girl I hate the most in my school. Today he gave me the silent treatment. (Sigh.)*

When this sweet seventh grader and my teenage self tried to force our fairy tales, we were acting more like orphans than adopted daughters of God (see Romans 8:14–17). We mistakenly thought we had to fend for ourselves. Can you believe it—princesses of the King acting like poor beggars?

Why Not Pursue Him?

When I'm tempted to act like a beggar or an orphan and force my fairy tale, here are four truths I often come back to. I pray they spare you the frustration and heartache I experienced.

1. *You are already loved completely and unconditionally.* You no longer have to fight for attention or find your worth in a boyfriend. Listen to how deeply—and how long—the King has loved you: "I have loved you with an everlasting love; I have drawn you with loving-kindness" (Jeremiah 31:3 NIV).

2. *You don't know what is best for you, but God does.* Have you ever set your sights on a guy only to realize later he's totally wrong for you? I've done that more times than I care to count (like on that plane). That's because: "Desire without knowledge is not good, and whoever makes haste with his feet misses his way" (Proverbs 19:2). God, unlike us, knows everything. Including the hearts of all guys (1 Kings 8:39). You can trust Him to lead and protect you, His princess daughter, even when you don't realize you need protecting.

3. *You're not actually waiting on a guy to pursue you—you're waiting on God.* Whenever you're frustrated over how long it's taking a guy to notice you, remember God is in control of everything: "The king's heart is a stream of water in the hand of the Lord; he turns it wherever he will" (Proverbs 21:1). If the Lord can move the heart of the most powerful man in the land, He can turn any guy's heart. Wait for His perfect timing.

4. *God has nothing but good in store for those who wait on Him.* You can rest easy. Psalm 25:3 says: "None who wait for you shall be put to shame." That's a fact you can count on from your God

who makes promises and keeps them. Of course, that doesn't mean we'll always get what we want when we want it. God tells us that in this world we will have trouble. But ultimately, in the end, He will work everything together for the good of those who love Him (Romans 8:28).

What Will It Be?

In a few years, after reading Matthew 16:25, I would write:

I only have two choices, don't I?
1. Try to save my life by forcing a fairy tale and end up losing my life, or
2. Lose my life by forfeiting the fairy tale and end up finding my life.

But until then, I kept trying to force my fairy tale. I'd chase down love, and as soon as I got remotely close, I'd panic and run the other direction. Find out why in the next chapter.

YOUR JOURNAL CORNER

How are you trying to force a fairy tale?
Which of the four truths from this chapter
encourages you the most to trust King
Jesus with your love life?
What girls are you especially jealous of?
Would you write out a prayer for them
right now, that they would use their
personality, gifts, and looks to make
much of God?

running from love

Have you ever watched *Runaway Bride*? Julia Roberts stars as Maggie Carpenter, a confused woman who repeatedly ditches her fiancé the day of the wedding. She just freaks out and runs. It used to be my favorite movie, probably because I could relate to Maggie.

No, I was never engaged, but I did run—over and over—as soon as a relationship was about to take off. I won't bore you with all my running stories, but here's one.

Getting My Running Shoes On

Bennett first noticed me the day I talked about my trip to Israel in a college chapel service. It wasn't long before we were studying together and having fun, meaningful conversation at Starbucks, the Bourgeois Pig Café, and McCormick & Schmick's. He even did melt-your-heart things like leaving candy at the receptionist desk for me.

About a month later, he invited me to a botanical garden

and out to dinner with another couple. It sounded romantic. You'd think I'd have been jumping up and down and calling all my friends, but instead I declined his invitation and promptly grabbed my running shoes.

I called one of his friends to see if I was right about him wanting more than friendship. Yep, Bennett did want more. When Bennett's friend sensed my hesitation, she tried to help by saying, "Ask yourself if you'd be sad or okay if he were moving to Florida right now and you might not see him again."

I think she thought I'd want him to stay. But I wanted him to go to Florida. Suddenly I was fine with never seeing him again. In fact, I was desperate to get him out of my life that night.

So I did. I called Bennett at 11:15 p.m. and asked if we could talk. He came to my dorm lobby right away and was out of my life within minutes.

The next day, the drastic thing I had done began to sink in. My journal entry shows my pain and confusion:

> *I want to cry every time I see Bennett. What is he thinking? I don't know why I hurt so much—I don't think I like him. I feel like I'll never learn to love.*

Filled to the Brim with Fear

Two months before, I'd started to realize—and record—my issues:

> *Mom teased me this morning about liking guys until they like me and then dropping them because I don't like them any-*

more. I always thought it was because I hadn't yet found "the right one." But I don't think that's true. I am too insecure. I fill my résumé with activities to try to boost my confidence. But it never works. I believe that if I went out with a guy and he really got to know me, he'd reject me. So, instead, I suddenly lose interest.

After I graduated from college, I did manage to get a tad further with another relationship. After a couple of dates with Joe, I wrote:

I guess we decided we're dating. We're going to continue, and time will tell. I'm filled to the brim with fear.

As I continued journaling that week, I began to understand myself better:

Who would've known I had so many fears? There's something about a guy pursuing me that scares me tremendously. I'm fine as long as there's some distance between us. But whenever I sense true love and care from a guy, I want to run away as quickly as possible.

God, You say perfect love casts out fear. But I'm seeing that I have layers and layers of fear. Why?

I believe I have to be strong, that a guy will love me only if he sees my strength rather than my tears. I'm afraid to show Joe my heart, afraid of being rejected.

You probably won't be surprised to learn my running shoes were kicking up dust in Joe's face within the month. Ironic, huh? I never got what I wanted most, because I feared not getting it. (If you're scratching your head trying to make sense of my convoluted brain, don't even bother trying!)

Love Solid and Deep as an Iceberg

Years later—after a guy rejected me—I wrote the following based on 1 John 4 and Ephesians 3:17–19:

I will live like I am deeply loved this year. As I write this resolution, my head nods yes and my heart screams no. Connect my head and my heart, God who is love.

You outdid Yourself the day You sent Your only Son into this world so I might have life through Him. And all this evidence of love mounted up when I didn't even care for You in the first place.

Surely You, the God with scars, won't be surprised when I tell You that life's not fair, and people wound, and I often feel more afraid than deeply loved.

You whisper that perfect love casts out fear. And isn't that what Your love is? Perfect? Solid as the thickest, deepest, most immense iceberg off the coast of Antarctica?

And didn't I just read that usually only one-ninth of an iceberg is visible above water? So it must be that I have seen only the tip—the smallest tip—of the iceberg of Your love.

Root and ground me in this unbelievable love of Jesus so I can began to understand how wide and deep and high and long it is. Do this, and I will float calm and unafraid on the iceberg of Your love.

The God with Scars

Speaking of Jesus' deep, deep love, I'm curious. Have you ever thought about the fact that Jesus has scars? The Bible talks about His five crucifixion scars: one on each hand and one on each foot where the nails pinned Him to that tree. And one in His side where a soldier pierced Him with a spear to make sure He was good and dead.

And He was. That's why His followers were so terrified when He appeared to them three days later. Thomas wasn't there that day, so his friends stumbled all over themselves telling him what he had missed. Thomas said, "Unless I see in his hands the mark of the nails, and place my finger into the mark of the nails, and place my hand into his side, I will never believe" (John 20:25).

He wanted proof. Visible proof. So eight days later, Jesus found Thomas. He said, "Put your finger here, and see my hands; and put out your hand, and place it in my side. Do not disbelieve, but believe." And when Thomas saw Jesus' scars, he breathed, "My Lord and my God!" (verses 27–28).

I love what Jesus said next, because He was talking about you and me: "Have you believed because you have seen me? Blessed are those who have not seen and yet have believed" (verse 29).

Do You Believe?

So what about you? Do you believe in this Jesus who died over two thousand years ago, was raised from the dead three days later, and is seated at the right hand of God this very moment? Will you believe that He was pierced for your sins? If so, Isaiah 53:5 says He was punished to bring you peace with God, and His wounds heal you from the disease of sin (including fear).

Are you, like I was, deathly afraid of being rejected? Of being hurt? We live in a world affected by sin, with people who have all been born with a sin nature. This means we will be hurt and disappointed by every single human being we meet. It's only a matter of time.

But there is one who knows what it is to be wounded, who was scarred in our place. I pray that if you don't already, you come to know and believe the great love He has for you. Then you will be able to live unafraid.

I'm not saying I don't have any more fears. But God has significantly freed me. He sure did it in a surprising way though—by allowing me to experience rejection and then helping me through it. I know that sounds crazy, but I think you'll understand when I tell you about it in chapters 13 and 15.

For now, though, stick with me as I share how I tried to fix my messed-up self (think, wishing I could become a nun, and so much more!). And if you're thinking this all sounds rather obsessive, you're right. I was obsessed.

That's why I'm writing this book—the good, the bad, and the ugly—beginning with the bad and the ugly. Stick with me on this journey, though, and we'll get to the good. I promise. God's into the business of miracles, and He sure worked one when He changed me from the inside out. And He can do it in you too, you know!

YOUR JOURNAL CORNER

Write about a time you ran from a relationship. What specific fear caused you to run? How does Jesus' immense love for you take away your fears?

CHAPTER 9

the broken fix-it woman

As I slipped from my teen years into my twenties, I realized increasingly that I had serious problems or, at least, serious pain. Naturally, being the independent young woman I was, I tried to fix it. The tools in my belt ranged from busying myself, to ignoring guys, to refusing to hope (it's safer that way), to lying to myself as I did in my journal here:

> *I don't want to like him. I don't want to be hurt. I know! I'll tell myself he just cares about money. After all, his sister said he's driven. I know I'm judging him. But I have to guard my always-imaginative, scheming, scared heart.*

Where's the Closest Convent?

Becoming a nun was probably my craziest fix-it scheme. It sure sounded easier than dealing with real life. As a twenty-year-old college student I wrote:

Steve asked if I wanted to study with him and a few others at a coffee shop. I did and struggled so much. I know he's getting together with Megan, but when I look in his eyes, I'm extremely attracted to him. He touches me, leans in when talking, and flirts. He tickled me and held out my coat for me to put my arms in. I want to scream at him to stop, but it's my problem. I wish I could go to a convent and be a nun.

Since I didn't know of any convents in the area, I turned to hate. After all, you can't love someone when you're busy hating them!

Loving—Then Hating—That Guy

I could flip the switch from love to hate in a matter of seconds, like this:

I put a picture in Kevin's mailbox with a compliment I'd heard about him. That night, I brought my pictures to supper to show him. I casually asked who he had invited to the Junior/Senior Banquet. I could feel my smile and movements freeze as he told me her name is Alicia. She is very popular. My heart went cold.

He kept making corny jokes while looking at my photo album. I told him he was annoying. I had already begun hating him—the only way I knew to recover my heart. I was dull and numb the whole night and went to bed with no hope.

Band-Aid Fixes

But all my attempts to fix myself were like slapping a flimsy Band-Aid on a deep, gaping wound. I realized this when I wrote:

> *I keep trying to seal up my heart by ignoring and running from guys, but that doesn't mean I'm not thinking about them.*

Colossians 2:20–23 says the same thing. It explains that boundaries and rules aren't enough to stop me from doing wrong. On their own, they're not capable of getting to the root issue—they don't deal a deathblow to the old me.

Calling for Help

As I slowly began to realize that my attempts weren't curing my boy-craziness, I cried to God for help:

> *Once again I find myself drawn to a guy. God, I need You. I need You to set a seal over my heart and emotions. Fill the emptiness in my soul, Lord. I'm miserable without You. How do I get out of this mess? I want to climb out of the trap I'm in, but I can't see past these chains. You alone can rescue me. Please free me from this bondage. My heart won't stop craving and coveting men.*

Crying out to God for rescue was a good start, but I was still missing something—something huge.

Repentance: Counterfeit or the Real Deal?

I realize now that I was crying for help for all the wrong reasons. How do I know? I cried buckets of tears but not over the fact that I wasn't loving God with all my heart, soul, and mind, which Jesus says is the greatest commandment (Matthew 22:37). Nope, I cried because my heart ached, because I couldn't get what I wanted.

This is what 2 Corinthians 7:10 calls worldly sorrow that produces death. It's when we're sorry about our sin because we're dealing with its painful consequences, and we want life to be easier. Maybe we feel some guilt, but we have no intention of turning away from our sin. We might say we hate our sin, but we really love it. We pick it up, touch it, look at it, enjoy it. We fuel it. We might not even call it "sin."

Godly sorrow, on the other hand, "brings repentance that leads to salvation and leaves no regret" (NIV). *Repentance* is a big word that means making a one-eighty, turning from our sin to God. When God is the reason we hate our sin (rather than just the consequences we're facing), that's a great thing. Why? Because when we're truly repentant, God is deeply moved:

> Thus says the One who is high and lifted up,
>   who inhabits eternity, whose name is Holy:
> "I dwell in the high and holy place,
>   and also with him who is of a contrite and lowly spirit,
> to revive the spirit of the lowly,
>   and to revive the heart of the contrite." (Isaiah 57:15)

9: the broken fix-it woman

Break Me, Please!

In a couple of years I would write the following prayer in my journal. I'm sharing it here in the hopes that it will help you understand what real repentance might sound like. It's what I desperately needed at this point in my life but didn't yet understand:

God Most High,
Thank You that You're committed to giving me Yourself. You don't want me to find my happiness—nor can I—with anyone or anything less than You. Why do I think I know better than You what I need? I'm miserable in my strivings and resistance against You. Give me the gift of repentance.

I confess my lust toward men and relinquish to You the desire, need, and hope of marriage. I'm sorry for living for guys rather than for You. Break me over this sin, God.

I seem to think that my Creator, Father, and King is acting foolishly. I think I deserve more, that I'm pretty good. Who am I comparing myself to, God? Certainly not You. My heart is cold toward You. I want to be in control of my own life. I don't want You to be Lord of my life—I just want to use You to make me look good.

God, I step down from the throne of my life and invite—no, plead—with You to assume Your rightful place as Lord, as Boss. Forgive me. Thank You that You have.

Take my love, Lord, even though it is barely alive, and fan it into flame for You.

Broken Girl to Beautiful Trophy

But I'm jumping ahead. When I first cried out to the Healer in desperation, I had a breakdown—and a breakthrough—in a twelve-passenger van, and my life has never been the same since.

But before I take you on that road trip, let me encourage you that change *is* possible. No, you can't fix who you are on your own, but God is in the business of transforming broken girls into beautiful trophies of His grace. First, though, you need to be truly repentant.

Are you? If not, ask God to begin replacing your worldly sorrow with godly sorrow that leads to repentance. Ask Him to help you see your sinfulness as He sees it, to see His awesome holiness, and then to help you turn in faith to Jesus.

YOUR JOURNAL CORNER

What are some of the "tools" in your tool belt that you're using to try to fix yourself? What might godly sorrow and worldly sorrow look like in your life? Is there a sin you need to repent of now?

PART 2

The BREAKING and the REMAKING

(Relinquishing Control)

breakdown and breakthrough in a twelve-passenger van

When I asked God to break me, maybe I should've been more specific and asked that He do it when the guy I wanted to impress wasn't around.

Six months before, I'd graduated from a college with eight hundred guys and started a job at a women's ministry (you can imagine how many single guys were employed there). Pickings were slim, but still I managed to find a guy to set my sights on.

John was a shipping clerk, and like Caleb (from chapter 6), he seemed too focused on God (and the mail) to notice girls. The thrill of a challenge—along with the fact that he wrote poetry—

was enough to send my heart pitter-pattering.

You can imagine my excitement when we signed up for the same storm-relief trip.

Still Striving for Perfection

While we were busy picking up marooned toasters, door knobs, and other storm-tossed debris, I tried not to even think about John, but it didn't work. I not only thought about him, I tried to get his attention. One night I wrote:

> *Everything God has given me I use as props in a giant, self-glorifying production.*
> *My beauty I use to draw men's hearts after me.*
> *My piano-playing I use to set myself above other pianists.*
> *My speaking and writing I use to establish a name for myself.*
> *I wear modest clothes but still long for guys to remember my image on the back of their eyelids even after I've left the room.*
> *I am Paula, the masquerading servant of God, who really longs to be God—to have everyone worship and adore me.*

I hated myself for it. It wasn't the first time I'd seen just how powerless I was to live the way God wanted me to. Sometime before, I'd written in my journal:

> *I wake up every morning thinking about my shortcomings the day before. I need to lighten up and enjoy life.*

10: breakdown—and breakthrough

Another time, after comparing myself to my friends and co-workers, I wrote:

> *I feel like my Christianity should look like Megan's, all bubbly, passionate, and exciting. At the same time, it should look like Trina's, disciplined and modest. And it should be like Sarah's —knowing Scripture backward and forward. Oh, yeah, while I'm at it, I should be like Kathy, pure and uninterested in the opposite sex. And I should definitely mentor someone. Is it any wonder I'm passionless and exhausted?*

I knew God requires perfection; I just couldn't figure out how to achieve it.

Twenty-Two Going on Seventy-Five

Years of trying to meet God's standards on my own finally caught up with me the day we traveled home. That morning I woke up with an overwhelming sense of despair like I'd never experienced. I knew that no matter how hard I tried, I wouldn't make it through the day without failing—I would end up wanting John more than God.

As we climbed into the twelve-passenger van, waves of emotional exhaustion broke over me. It was the worst time imaginable to have a meltdown, with so many of us crammed in that van and my crush right in front of me, but there was no holding back my sobs.

"God, if this is Christianity, I'm done," I breathed. I meant it. I got out my journal and wrote:

I feel like a seventy-five-year-old woman. I am so weary. I can't carry this load anymore.

Hearing a Brand-New Voice

And then I heard Him. Jesus. He spoke to me through Matthew 11:28–30: "Come to me, all who labor and are heavy laden, and I will give you rest. Take my yoke upon you, and learn from me, for I am gentle and lowly in heart, and you will find rest for your souls. For my yoke is easy, and my burden is light."

I'd heard about Jesus my whole life, but this was the first time I really heard Him. I finally realized that the hard, heavy burden I'd always known Christianity to be didn't line up one bit with His promise of peace and rest.

For the first time in my life I wondered, *Is it possible I might not be a Christian?* Suddenly, I wasn't sure anymore.

Old News Turned New

When I got back from that storm-relief trip, I began studying Romans 5–8 with two friends. What we read and discussed in those chapters changed my life. Some of it was old news. You know—Jesus came to earth, lived a perfect life, died on a cross, was buried in a tomb, rose from the dead three days later, and then went back to heaven. When I was growing up, I'd rehearsed the story every Sunday at the Communion table.

But I'd never connected the dots. I'd never understood how these facts about Jesus applied to me—how they changed everything about me.

It was the first time I realized Jesus did all this for me. I didn't have to perform for Him (as if I could!) but could rest in His performance on my behalf.

Jesus had made the Great Exchange that pitch-black afternoon over two thousand years ago when He cried, "It is finished," and gave up His life. He "wore" and completely did away with my sins so I might "wear" His righteousness forever. He experienced God's wrath and condemnation for my sins so I might never ever have to experience God's anger or displeasure. And Jesus' resurrection from the dead proved that God had accepted this amazing transaction.

But that wasn't all.

A Whole New Me

My whole life I'd struggled to defeat the power of sin—with no success. But now I was reading startling truths I'd never grasped.

It wasn't just Jesus who had died—I'd died with Him. It wasn't just Jesus who had been buried—my old self, packed with sin, had been buried with Him, too. And when Jesus burst out of that tomb with brand-new resurrection life, I, too, was given new life! Galatians 2:20 sums it up well:

> I have been crucified with Christ. It is no longer I who live, but Christ who lives in me. And the life I now live in the flesh I live by faith in the Son of God, who loved me and gave himself for me.

For the first time, I understood that Jesus didn't die to forgive me of my sin but leave me in it. He died to forgive and to free me from the power of sin. Suddenly I realized I didn't have to be jealous of that pretty girl. I didn't have to covet every guy I saw. I didn't have to hate that guy for not liking me. I wasn't powerless anymore.

In fact, in Christ I was no longer that helpless, hopeless, boy-crazy girl. I had a new identity now: I was dead to sin, alive to God, and in Christ Jesus. My only job? Believing it to be so and living in light of that truth.

From that point on, I saw God begin to change not only my outward behavior but even the hidden desires of my heart. Whether I actually became a Christian at this time or not, I can't say. I asked Jesus to save me at about age four, but this was the first time I really understood why the Good News was such good news!

This was the beginning of my whole new life.

Notice I said "the beginning." It's not like I was instantly transformed. But as I remembered, believed, and personalized these truths, my overwhelming despair ebbed away and was gradually replaced by hope. I stopped trying so hard and just started dying. Or rather, I started believing that I had already died with Christ. I gave up control and let Jesus take over.

And boy, did He have a lot of cleanup work to do in me, just as I'd done on that storm-relief trip.

Little Did I Know . . .

Remember my van ride home? My friend—the one who would later marry John—let me listen to a song on her iPod called "Acres of Hope" by Shane & Shane. I listened over and over through my headphones as they sang the story of Hosea 2, the story of how God's people left Him for other lovers, and of how He would woo them back to Himself. These lyrics quieted my sobs and spoke tenderly to my beat-up heart:

He will allure her
He will pursue her
And call her out
To wilderness with flowers in His hand
She is responding
Beat up and hurting
Deserving death
But offerings of life are found instead. . . .
How the story ends is
Love and tenderness in Him
Not safe, but worth it.[7]

Little did I know that in the years ahead Jesus was going to allure me into the wilderness and speak tenderly to me there.

First, though, He had another important lesson to begin teaching me. I needed to start learning what true love really is.

YOUR JOURNAL CORNER

If you belong to Jesus, how has He transformed you *from the inside out*? If you're truly a Christian, you'll be able to say, "This was me before Christ, and this is the radically different person I am today after Christ." If you don't see Him changing you at your core, would you ask Him to show you if you really know Him?

you want me to love him more?

I'd been at my job for a short time when Jack began helping my company with their IT needs on a temporary basis. He was in and out of the office, but we hit it off right away and were soon good friends. Having a close friendship with a guy I liked was new for me. Usually I liked guys from a distance.

Over the next few months, Jack started hanging out with me and my friends, and I often found myself asking God for a pure heart:

> *Teach me how to be a friend without trying to seduce Jack. I've been using my eyes and smile to get his attention, but I give these to You, God. Give me an undivided heart that beats to know You more completely. Rescue me, Jesus!*

One Friend Too Many

I wonder now if Jack's friendship with my roommate, Carrie, was part of Jesus' surprising rescue. Things got tense in our little home when Jack moved into our neighborhood and jealousy moved into my heart. Sometimes it seemed I came out on top, but other times Jack seemed to prefer Carrie:

> *I had so much fun sitting by Jack at the play last night. But today I overheard him talking with Carrie and felt that old familiar twinge of jealousy.*

Still, I was filled with hope as weeks passed and the memories grew: Jack tickling the bottom of my ballet slipper on the ride home from a costume party; Jack and I splashing each other on a canoe ride; Jack leaving an "Eight Reasons Paula's My Friend" list in my car. One day I wrote,

> *I'm in deep and can't stop grinning. I think I have Jack-itis.*

I didn't realize what harm my Jack-itis could do until I met Hezekiah and Merodach-Baladan.

Come on In!

Don't worry, Hezekiah and Merodach-Baladan aren't two *more* guys I fell for. They're actually two guys in the Bible.

Have you heard the story of the teenager Daniel and his people, the Israelites, being taken captive by the king of Babylon? What you might not know is that one hundred years before, King Hezekiah made a deadly mistake that led to this disaster.

It happened the day Prince Merodach-Baladan from Babylon sent men loaded down with letters and a gift to Hezekiah, the

Israelite king. Hezekiah was so flattered by this attention from a potential enemy that he didn't stop and think.

> Hezekiah welcomed them gladly. And he showed them his treasure house, the silver, the gold, the spices, the precious oil, his whole armory, all that was found in his storehouses. There was nothing in his house or in all his realm that Hezekiah did not show them. (Isaiah 39:2)

After reading this, I wrote in my journal:

> *Like Hezekiah, my "walls" are down and my "gate" is open. I'm welcoming Jack in to look at all my treasures. He is consuming my heart and stealing my affection from You, God. Would You teach me what it means to guard my heart?*

A Conversation in the Cherry Orchard

I had never understood what people meant when they told me to "guard my heart," but suddenly it was important to figure it out. So I took a walk through a cherry orchard and asked God to help me understand. Here's what I learned:

1. Guarding my heart (my mind, will, and emotions) does not mean protecting myself from being hurt. There's no way I can insulate myself from any possibility of pain. It's a regular part of relationships in this broken world.
2. Guarding my heart does mean loving God most. It means keeping the first commandment first—loving Him with all

my heart, soul, mind, and strength (Mark 12:30).

While that was helpful, it didn't mean I suddenly stopped liking Jack. Oh, I tried. I gave myself all kinds of reasons to stop.

First, I told myself Jack wasn't available, but that lasted a whoppin' three days because . . . technically he *was* available!

Then I decided to focus on the fact that it obviously wasn't God's will for us to be together. If He wanted us together, we would be.

But finally I realized, no, that's not it either. It was God's will for us to be friends. I had just endured our friendship because I wanted more, but now I realized our friendship was a gift to be embraced.

The Secret of True Love

Soon after that revelation I had another one:

> *I don't need to love Jack less; I need to love him more, with Christ's love. I realize I have not really loved him; I have loved myself.*

How did I know this? Lean in close, 'cause you won't hear this true-love secret from the world. It's found in 1 John 3:16: "This is how we know what love is: Jesus Christ laid down his life for us. And we ought to lay down our lives for our brothers" (NIV).

Jesus showed us the ultimate picture of true love when He died to save us from sin. While we probably won't ever physically die to save someone's life (the greatest sign of love), all true love involves a "death" or sacrifice of some sort—like our time or our preferences.

As 1 Corinthians 13:4–5 says, "Love is patient and kind; love does not envy or boast; it is not arrogant or rude. It does not insist on its own way; it is not irritable or resentful." Anything less than what's best for the other person isn't true love—it's a selfish counterfeit.

The Celebration Journal

That same day, Jack sent me a link to a video about a baby named Eliot, who wasn't supposed to survive his birth. But when he did, Eliot's parents celebrated each day they had with him until he died ninety-nine days later.

That's when I decided I would do the same thing with Jack's friendship. I would embrace it with a "celebration journal" and focus on loving Jack with God's love:

Day 2: Celebrating that I was able to make my friend molasses cookies for his trip. He sent a text later, saying, "The cookies are perfect!"

Day 4: Celebrating the distance and silence today, knowing these are necessary and healthy in any relationship. Celebrating the fact that God is in control and that Jack is enjoying a change of scenery in Florida.

Day 7: Celebrating (against my natural inclination) the truth that sharing my friend is a good thing. So I celebrate the fact

*that Jack and Carrie are at the park together. Carrie needs
good friends right now.*

Surprising Release

As I continued to celebrate Jack's friendship, something crazy-unexpected happened:

*I don't know how, but I don't want Jack romantically anymore.
I don't know if it's because I'm not flirting with him or because
God has become more sweet to me recently.*

The last entry in my celebration journal read,

*I celebrate the fact that You're doing what I couldn't do, God.
You're releasing me from my strong desire for Jack.*

Little did I know, my desire for Jack was nothing compared to
what I would feel when Edward entered and rocked my world.

YOUR JOURNAL CORNER

What do you need to do to guard your heart, not to protect yourself from pain but to love God more?
Are you embracing your friendships with guys or enduring them because you want more? Based on 1 John 3:16,
how can you better love—truly love— the guys around you?

CHAPTER 12

when you get what you want but it's all wrong

I've always been friendly and outgoing, so it was no big deal to introduce myself to the new guy at church. It was a big deal, however, to invite him the next Sunday to join my brother and me for lunch at Steak 'n Shake. If I'd been honest with myself, I would have admitted that it was a brazen attempt to go out with an intriguing guy, and I would have resisted the urge.

But sometimes we'd rather lie to ourselves and do what *we* want than admit the truth and *not* do what we want. So I convinced myself this lunch was all about letting my brother hang out with an older, godly guy.

I don't know what my brother thought, but by the time I'd finished slurping down—or was it drooling in—my cookies 'n cream milkshake, Edward was my Idol with a capital *I*. Never mind that Proverbs 19:2 warns: "Desire without knowledge is not good, and whoever makes haste with his feet misses his way."

All I knew was that Edward's grasp of the Word of God was amazing. Who talks about obscure books from the Old Testament in a way that's totally applicable to real life? I was a goner.

"Whatever It Takes, God"

Not long after that, Edward asked if I'd be interested in helping him in ministry. My pastor agreed it was an incredible opportunity but warned me to guard my heart against romantic attachment. "Unless Edward tells you otherwise," he said, "it's all about the mission for him."

His words were about two weeks too late.

As Edward and I began ministering together, I was filled with fear that I wasn't good enough or deep enough for him. (That, by the way, should have stopped me in my tracks. It just doesn't work to be afraid of the guy you like.) Edward seemed so far above me. But he also seemed to like me.

That is, at least, until a comment of mine revealed that even though we are both Christians, we approach life as differently as two committed Christians could. And right then it was as if a giant wall appeared between us. At the time, I didn't know what had built that wall, but two days later I wrote:

> Edward must be removed from first place in my heart. Forgive me, God, for crying tears of pain and grief for myself rather than tears of repentance for having worshiped and loved a man more than You, the majestic, merciful God of the universe.

12: when you get what you want

Free me from my idol. Do whatever it takes to be first in my heart and life. Make me wholly, joyfully, unreservedly Yours.

Do you remember my desperate prayer from chapter 1, that God would do whatever it took to free me from my idol? This was that same prayer.

God Prepares Me for the Storm

God was about to answer my prayer, but He knew I needed to be grounded in His Word in order to survive the impending storm. In His kindness, He laid it on my heart to begin getting up earlier each morning to soak in His Word—a big deal for a girl who needs oodles of sleep! As it turned out, I made that decision not a minute too soon.

In the words of Randy Alcorn, "Suffering will come; we owe it to God, ourselves, and those around us to prepare for it," rather than trying to figure it out "on the fly, at a time when our thinking is muddled and we're exhausted."[8]

So how should we prepare? Randy Alcorn asked this of Darrell Scott, the father of seventeen-year-old Rachel, the first victim of the Columbine High School shooting. Without hesitation Mr. Scott answered, "Become a student of God's Word."[9]

I'm in no way comparing my pain with the pain of the Scotts. But no matter how small or great our pain, I'm convinced suffering will come to all of us—and that Mr. Scott's answer is *the* answer: "Become a student of God's Word."

Are you?

How to Begin
Becoming a Student of God's Word

Studying the Word of God is so important because it's the way God promises to communicate to us today. Here are a few things to consider as you get started:

- Plan ahead. Choose a quiet place and a time to meet with God in His Word and in prayer. Then, find a reading plan (you can search for one on the Internet) and stick with it rather than hopping around.

- Pray before you start. Ask God to open your eyes to help you see wonderful things in His Word (Psalm 119:18). Pray as you read. Pray what you read into your life and the lives of those around you.

- Study God through His Word the way you'd study a guy you like—wanting to know everything about him. Jesus tells us that all of Scripture—even the law and the prophets—point to Him (Luke 24:27). Look for Jesus as you read! Learn what He's like.

- If you feel like you're in over your head, ask a wise, older Christian to help you get started.

The point isn't just to stuff a bunch of information into your head but to get to know God's heart and allow Him to change yours through His living, active Word (Hebrews 4:12).

A Long, Lonely Season

As I started digging into God's Word, He began to give me more of a desire to surrender to His plan for my life. And just in time, because shortly after I learned Edward would be leaving for several months. The day he left town, I wrote:

> *It's difficult to accept this loneliness. Still, I choose to run to You, God, surrendering in spite of the pain.*

That wasn't the first or the last time. Day after day I chose to surrender to God and His plan for my life. I yielded on the days I just wanted to kick Edward, and I yielded on the days when all I wanted was to be near Edward. During that lonely season, I learned that surrender isn't a one-time event but a moment-by-moment choice.

Five long months passed before Edward returned. When he asked to get together to talk about ministry, my parents and close friends advised me not to meet with him alone, in order to keep guarding my heart. So even though I wanted to, I didn't meet with him alone.

Soon after, the plot thickened when my sister and I left on vacation to visit a friend on the West Coast. The last thing I expected was to hit it off with another guy.

Sparks Fly at Stella's Café

But I did. The evening my friend invited several of her friends to Stella's Café, I ended up sitting across from Daniel. When he mentioned he'd lived in another country for years, I asked how that had made him the person he is today. My question startled him, and my friends laughingly explained, "Paula's the queen of questions."

"I'm the king of questions!" he grinned. And with that, the sparks flew. We wanted to know as much about each other as possible. Daniel sent a Facebook friend request that night, and we exchanged fun messages over the next month.

And then he asked if he could call me. Our relationship was obviously about to go deeper, and I was excited. After all, Edward and I were barely even talking.

When You Get What You Want

That first phone call with Daniel went better than I could've imagined. He was funny, complimentary, and smart. But of all things, while we were talking, I got a call on the other line from Edward.

He wanted to know if we could get together to talk about possibly pursuing more than friendship. He'd been praying about it for a while and knew I might need to pray about it, too.

"I don't need to pray about it," I responded. I had been waiting for this moment for almost a year. Scratch that—for my whole life!

After we met, though, he wasn't sure if he should move forward. I wrote:

> *The desire was so sharp between us tonight I could've cut it with a knife. And yet things are so complicated. He realized*

during our talk that I'm nowhere near his lifestyle of hanging out with non-Christians and engaging with their music and movies.

But that night he called and said he wanted to pursue a relationship, even knowing our differences. I was on top of the world. For one day.

But It's All Wrong

And then reality set in. After ice cream and a walk around the lake with Edward, I wrote:

I feel like I'm on trial, being measured to fit Edward's mold. I'm excited about entering his world but only if I can enter as Paula. I feel like I have to perform for him spiritually.

A few days later, Edward and I realized that we'd never really been friends—just ministry partners. So we decided to work on our friendship, both hoping it would grow into more.

Because of the recent turn of events, I knew I needed to tell Daniel about Edward. After I did, I wrote in my journal:

Both relationships are back in Your hands where they belong, God. I fear I'll lose them both, but if I gain more of You in the process, what will it matter?

I seemed so close to what I'd always wanted. God had sent not one but two guys who were interested in me. And yet I was about to enter the darkest time of my life. It would be "a severe mercy" —a painful season I would thank God for later.

YOUR JOURNAL CORNER

How can you get serious about becoming a student of God's Word now so you're prepared for the suffering that will inevitably come your way? Spend a few minutes working on your plan and share it with a friend who will help you stick to it.

a shattered dream: winter in my soul

Y ou poor girl!" began Daniel's compassionate voice mail in response to my dilemma about him and Edward. He said several sweet things and then asked me to call him, ending with a mysterious, "You don't even know my story."

When I returned his call, Daniel told me he had been married for seven long, hard years—and was now divorced. I sure hadn't seen that coming! After I hung up, I wrote in my journal:

> *Right now, I would actually choose Daniel over Edward—even with his past, that is, if I knew You were okay with it, Lord. I've never felt so cherished, treasured, and loved by a man. Please help me trust and obey You no matter what You want me to do.*

Searching for God's View

I had to try to understand God's thoughts about marriage, divorce, and remarriage. I knew Christians had all kinds of different opinions, but only God's view mattered. I pulled out my Bible, told God I would listen to whatever He said, and looked up every reference I could find on marriage, divorce, and remarriage.

What I found took my breath away. I had grown used to our culture's acceptance of divorce and remarriage. But as I pored over God's Word, I was gripped by just how sacred, serious, and binding the marriage covenant is. It seemed clear, at least to me, that:

- God designed marriage as a tangible picture to showcase His love for His bride, the church (Ephesians 5:22–33).

- Divorce tells a lie about God's never-giving-up love for us. This is why He hates divorce—He will never leave us, His dearly loved bride (Malachi 2:13–16; Matthew 19:3–11).

- There's only one possible reason God seems to allow for divorce, and that's when one spouse breaks their covenant promise by having sex with someone other than their spouse (Matthew 5:32).

- Although God may allow for divorce in cases of adultery, He doesn't want that spouse to remarry but to remain single or be reunited with their spouse (1 Corinthians 7:10–11).

13: a shattered dream

So I told Daniel goodbye, and God gave me the grace not to look back.

My relationship with Edward, on the other hand, dragged on much longer.

Some wise friends saw what was happening and told me I needed to move on. Although my heart wasn't there at all, I took their counsel, hoping my emotions would catch up soon. I told Edward I was moving on and made my decision sound final.

After that conversation, though, I couldn't shake the fear that I'd just messed everything up.

The End—or the Beginning?

A few weeks later, I told Edward I hadn't meant to slam the door shut forever. But he no longer had hope for us. It was over. Soon after I wrote in my journal:

> I woke up missing Edward so much my inside hurt. Thank You that You are in control of this madness, God. I just read Elisabeth Elliot's thoughts about how a baby is born.[10] He is content, safe, and warm until suddenly he is forced from his home. He is pinched and squeezed and pushed until finally he is catapulted into a huge, cold, foreign world. He feels alone, and yet, if he clung to "life" as he has known it and doesn't take this path of "death," he'll never experience real life. Let me not resist this "death," God, this new beginning.

As God wooed me through my pain, I realized He loved me

too much to be satisfied with anything less than every square inch of me:

> *I had no idea when I decided to follow You, Jesus, that it would be so costly. That I'd have to bear in my body the "marks of Jesus Christ." I know I'm not being tortured physically, but You've put Your finger on what is dearest and closest to my heart—the dream of marriage and ministry with a man who is wholeheartedly following You. May this suffering refine me so I resemble You, my ever-loving, humble, suffering God.*

One day on the heels of autumn, a dear friend handed me a burlap bag filled with three tulip bulbs and told me we were going to "plant hope." So we did. We dug three holes beneath the tree in my front yard and buried the bulbs deep.

Days, weeks, and months passed. The leaves of that tree fell. The snow blew in and piled up. Life continued to feel dark and hopeless. Some days I remembered those tulip bulbs buried in the frozen soil of my front yard, and I anticipated the day God would bring them—and me—back to life.

Personalizing and Clinging to His Word

"What brings relief to your pain?" another friend asked me during that dark season.

My first thought was, "Nothing," but I paused, realizing God's promises had carried me through that long winter.

"God's Word," I answered. That night I wrote in my journal:

13: a shattered dream

Surprisingly, when I "should be" questioning and doubting Your love, God, I'm becoming more aware of it. How can that be?

Mainly, I was beginning to personalize and cling to God's words. I'd heard and read about Him my whole life. But it's one thing to know truth about God and another altogether to let Him be that truth to you every minute, every day.

Each Sunday when I saw Edward at church, I repeated Romans 8:31 over and over, reminding myself: "If God is for [me], who can be against [me]?" As a result of what felt like rejection from Edward, God was teaching me to delight in Him rather than in everything but Him.

I was learning, in the words of Pastor Tullian Tchividjian, that *Jesus + Nothing = Everything.*[11] I wrote:

> *All my life it's been God + _____: God + a relationship. God + health. God + a church where I feel respected and helpful. God + a schedule overflowing with activities. You've always been there, God, but I've really sought my happiness in everything but You. Thank You for answering my prayer that I'd be desperate for You. Thank You for continuing to destroy my idols. Thank You for the pressure You're applying to make me more like Jesus.*

Hope Springing Up

And you know what? Gradually I saw just how bad a match Edward and I would have been. I began to see that human rejection can be God's divine protection. And I realized that I hadn't messed up God's plan for my life. I wasn't nearly big enough to do that! (And neither are you.)

In fact, that winter God was preparing me for one of His good plans for my life. It was during this time that a dream took root and grew—a dream of one day writing a book for other boy-crazy girls. I knew I was nowhere near ready to write it yet, but my journals were filling with prayers that God would someday let me write just such a book.

I continued to personalize and cling to God's Word while slowly that long winter freeze began to melt into spring. One morning I spotted three shoots pushing their way up into the sunlight. My heart leapt, and I exclaimed to myself, "Hope is springing up!"

YOUR JOURNAL CORNER

**What truth about who God is do you need
to personalize right now?
Have you ever been tempted to think you
messed up God's plan for your life, and
why can that simply not be true?
If you've experienced rejection, how might
that also have been God's protection?**

CHAPTER 14

the knock on my door

Y ou need to put yourself out there," my friend coached me. "It's not like a guy will just knock on your front door." Except that's exactly what happened. Well, technically, he knocked on the back door. And he wasn't looking for me—he was thinking about buying my rental house.

After that visit, Jim started calling with questions about the house. He'd ask about the fridge or the dryer, and then after a long awkward pause, we'd talk about anything and everything but the house. For years, I'd admired Jim from afar for his prayer life and his purity, so I was excited to get to know him better. (He lived nearby, but I didn't see him often because he traveled most of the year on business.)

During this time, I was learning that God created men to initiate and pursue and women to wait and respond. So as my friendship with Jim grew—with lots of prayer and accountability—I didn't manipulate or initiate anything (a miracle for me!). But I also made plenty of mistakes along the way.

Let the Waiting Begin

All too soon, it was time for Jim to leave for another long business trip. It had been a sweet summer of friendship. After he left I wrote:

> *I'm having a hard time letting Jim go. I feel the loss already. I don't understand Your timing, God. I thought You were bringing us together. But now I get to trust You in a whole new way.*

Did I ever. For three months I heard nothing from Jim. You can imagine my excitement when I got a text in early December, saying, "Hey, Paula! What's your schedule like Tuesday? I'd like to get together." Could it be that Jim was ready to pursue me?

Nope. That was the first of many false alarms, where Jim would come home, ask to hang out, and then leave again with no explanation as to his intentions.

That December, I learned from Jim's close friend that Jim had just finished a forty-day fast, asking God if he should be married or single. Unfortunately, he still didn't feel like he had an answer. Jim's friend encouraged me to give Jim a few more months to figure it out and left me with the assurance that Jim cherished my friendship and was interested in me.

Words that Cut Like a Knife

That's why it was so hard to make sense of Jim's phone call two months later when he asked if it would be okay if he called and texted me. I hesitated, reminding him that I wanted to guard my heart for my future husband. I wasn't sure I should have a deep, intentional friendship with a guy who wasn't interested in marriage. He understood and shot straight: "I don't have any intention of pursuing you."

His words cut like a knife. I wanted so badly to ask him to clarify, "Ever? Or just now?" But I didn't. Somehow I heard myself respond mechanically, "I'll try and just be your friend." I went with it because I was certain he meant he had no intention of pursuing me *now*, but that he would soon.

So instead of climbing off that emotional roller-coaster ride when he told me he had no intention of pursuing me, I continued to ride it 'round and 'round and 'round.

My parents and friends encouraged me to just relax into my friendship with Jim. But I don't think they realized how sure I was that Jim would change his mind and pursue me before long.

That spring was filled with frustration as Jim's calls and texts were few and far between and not particularly satisfying.

When he returned that summer, I wrote:

If he'd pursue with gusto, he might be able to redeem himself.

Never mind that he'd already told me he had no intention of pursuing me. Like I said, I just knew he'd change his mind.

Back in the Game

And it looked as if he had in July when Jim brought me one of his mom's homemade strawberry pies, and we caught lightning bugs in glass jars. The next afternoon we, along with a couple of friends, ran and romped and splashed in a stream.

My euphoric feeling didn't last long, though. Jim returned to his sporadic text messaging, and I returned to telling God:

> As much as I want to rise up and demand that Jim tell me what's going on, I'll wait for You.

Frustrated . . . Why?

Have you ever been there? So frustrated with a guy friend you could pull your hair out? Ironically, I thought I was being all spiritual by waiting for God to get Jim on the same page that God and I were on. But looking back, it wasn't spiritual at all. In fact, my feelings should have clued me in that I had dangerous unmet expectations simmering just under the surface. If I had really been cool with just being Jim's friend, I wouldn't have been so uptight.

If you're angry at that disinterested guy friend, you might ask yourself, is it because I expect more than friendship?

He's Just Not That into You

There's something else you should ask yourself if you're feeling frustrated. No girl wants to admit that any guy on the planet just isn't that into her. But the fact remains, it's hardwired in guys to go hard after the girl they want. So if he's dragging his feet, bravely ask yourself the question, "Could it be that he's just not that into me?" Here's some ways how you might know.

He's probably not that into you if:

14: the knock on my door

- He doesn't seem all that interested in getting to know you.

- When he actually does ask you a question, he doesn't seem to remember your answer.

- He only gives you enough attention to keep you wondering what he's thinking.

- He flat out tells you he doesn't plan on pursuing you.

- It's not obvious. If you wonder, he's probably not.

Make sure you're not imagining interest on his part just because:

- His friend told you he liked you. Maybe he did at first, but that doesn't mean he does now.

- You know he's a godly guy and are convinced he must just be praying about it. And praying and praying and praying . . .

- He wants to hang out with you (maybe you're just a fun girl to spend time with).

- You're doing everything God's way, so surely God will bless this relationship.

- He pays more attention to you than to any other girl (that still doesn't mean he wants more than friendship).

"I Will Fight for You"

Back to my roller-coaster ride with Jim. I grew hopeful once more when I turned the page in my daily Bible reading and came to Exodus 14:14: "The Lord will fight for you, and you have only to be silent." At the time, I thought this meant God was fighting for my future relationship with Jim. Now, though, I know God was fighting for my heart, not my romance.

I waited quietly until one humbling day in August. When Jim invited me to lunch, I assumed he was asking me on a date. But when Friday rolled around, he had forgotten all about it. After reminding him and then paying for our meal at McDonald's I thought, *This is all over*.

So after a lot of prayer and counsel, I finally sent him a Facebook message. I explained that our friendship had been unsettling, stressful, and frustrating—and why. I said I'd be happy to meet to talk about this or simply go our separate ways.

I figured this would be the end of our friendship.

Clouds Big with Blessing

Just before I pushed send, I took a walk with God. As I rounded the bend of the hill, I was singing these words:

Ye fearful saints, fresh courage take,
The clouds that you now dread
Are big with mercy, and will break
In blessings on your head.[12]

14: the knock on my door

That's when I saw it and gasped in wonder. A nearby storm front had caused the clouds to mushroom and mount up, sun-kissed in pink. I knew this glorious cloud display was for me. God was assuring me that what looked so fearful and bleak now would end in blessing.

And it did. When Jim and I met next, he told me he realized he didn't want to lose me, but he didn't feel he knew me well enough to knock my door down in pursuit. He asked if we could start over and reevaluate when he returned home in four months. He was interested and hoped this would lead to commitment. I wrote:

> WOW. I really thought this would end things, but now I wonder if it might actually start things.

Let's Get This Show on the Road

Finally! This was the conversation I'd desperately wanted for a year. But if I thought things would drastically change, I was wrong. Just one week later I wrote:

> Change me, God, or I will destroy a man by my expectations. I've been frustrated and angry tonight, thinking, Does Jim have a clue how to romance a woman? This—and his snail's pace—are enough to make me want to jump ship. But I remember what I read this morning in Titus 1. Romance and speed aren't the qualities You commend in a man. Jim has all that You value from the list in Titus 1, as far as I can tell.

Forgive me for thinking badly of him. Prepare me to bring a man like him good—and not harm—all the days of my life (Proverbs 31:12).

About a month later, Jim asked if I'd pray about visiting him on a business trip for a week in November. I could stay with his friends for the week, and Jim and I could hang out between meetings. That was a big move for Jim, and after praying, I said yes and asked God to give us clear direction for our relationship by the end of December.

Little did I know I wouldn't have to wait that long.

YOUR JOURNAL CORNER

Are you convinced God is in the process of bringing you and a certain guy together? What other reasons (besides romance) might He have for placing this guy in your life? Is there an emotional roller-coaster relationship in your life right now? If so, how can you climb off?

the part where everything's supposed to end happily ever after

The day I left to visit Jim, God kindly gave me a heads-up that His purposes—not mine—would be accomplished on this trip. I wrote:

> Thank You, God, that You can do all things, and that none of Your purposes can be thwarted (Job 42:2). Accomplish all Your purposes for this week—not mine or Jim's—but Yours.

I reminded myself of that truth all week long, as Jim and I didn't have much time together. He ended up having almost nonstop business meetings. On top of that, we both were laid up with the flu for a couple of days.

Still Waiting

I didn't want to leave without knowing Jim's take on our relationship. But, as much as I wanted answers, I really wanted him to initiate that conversation. And it just didn't happen.

After Jim saw me off the final day, he sent a sweet text. He told me not to worry—he just needed time with the Lord, as our relationship was an important matter and I was a special friend. Even with his text, that next week was hard. I wrote:

> *I miss him and want to be near him, and still I find myself waiting. God gave me Isaiah 28:16: "Whoever believes will not be in haste." Ouch! I'm in a hurry so I can stop trusting God and start trusting in the title "girlfriend."*

The Bomb on My World

But "girlfriend" wasn't to be. When Jim called, he told me I was incredible and had all the biblical qualities of a great wife. But then he hesitantly shared, "The spark comes and goes."

"Like, being attracted?" I asked incredulously.

"Yes, I'm sorry," he said. "I know every girl wants to be beautiful." I was stunned.

God gave me so much grace for that call, but, oh, I cried when I hung up. Jim's admission had exploded on my world like an unexpected bomb.

Still, Jim didn't want to lose my friendship. He planned to pray more and get back to me about where we should go from here. I prayed:

> *God, make it so clear if You want me to continue this relationship. Otherwise, I'm taking this as Your leading me out.*

Comfort and Direction from Isaiah

God did give me direction. But first He comforted me with Isaiah 43:1–5:

> Fear not [Paula], for I have redeemed you;
>   I have called you by name, you are mine.
> When you pass through the waters, I will be with you;
>   and through the rivers, they shall not overwhelm you;
> when you walk through the fire you shall not be burned,
>   and the flame shall not consume you.
> For I am the Lord your God,
>   the Holy One of Israel, your Savior. . . .
> You are precious in my eyes,
>   and honored, and I love you. . . .
> Fear not, for I am with you.

I was blown away by this language of love, by God's nearness and intimacy. It's not like I got this much out of His Word every day— there's just something about hard times when God seems extra near through His Word! As I kept reading, Isaiah 50:4–8 helped me know what to do next. I wrote in my journal:

I've been asking You what to do. I take from this passage that I'm not to resist the pain or be rebellious. You'll help me and will see to it that I will not ultimately be disgraced. I am to set my face like a flint and not look back. You will vindicate me in Your perfect time.

Thank You, Jesus, for Your example in undergoing the most unfair, disgraceful treatment without a word. You didn't defend Yourself; You just received it. All looked hopeless and lost, and then up from the grave You arose! You triumphed over death, and God exalted You to the highest place of honor.

Thank You for a chance to share in Your sufferings, Jesus. Just as Your humiliation brought life to many, may my humiliation do the same.

As I figure out what to say to Jim, if there is any pride, accusation, or defensiveness, reveal that, and I will not say it. Grant me genuine humility so You might be my sole Defender.

As I continued through Isaiah, I knew what I needed to do next: "Depart, depart, go out from there; . . . You shall not go out in haste, and you shall not go in flight, for the Lord will go before you, and the God of Israel will be your rear guard" (52:11–12). Although Isaiah isn't talking about guy/girl relationships here, these verses helped to confirm my decision.

That night, Jim texted that he was ready to talk today or tomorrow. Because I'd realized it was good not to hurry, I said tomorrow would be better.

Saying Goodbye

When Jim called, nothing had changed. He still wanted to be friends but wasn't ready to pursue anything more.

So I breathed a quick prayer for help and told Jim that since he wasn't ready to take the next step, I thought we should move on.

There was dead silence. It seemed he had not expected my response.

Once my words had settled in, I thanked Jim for the gift of his friendship. Through it I had learned to wait on God and to trust Him. It had also worked into me a gentle and quiet spirit that was so foreign to me (but oh-so-beautiful to God).

Jim remarked that my trust in the Lord was phenomenal; he prayed for us, and then we said goodbye.

As I grieved the loss of Jim's friendship and the hope for more, the realization settled in that trying to do things "right" hadn't guaranteed I'd get what I wanted. But I knew God was at work and that living under providence is a good place to be.

The Protection of God's Providence

Have you heard of God's providence before? It's a big theological word that means, according to Augustine, that "everything that happens does so because God wills it to happen, wills it to happen before it happens, wills it to happen in the way that it happens."[13]

Like me, you may not see what God is doing in the details of your story. But trust me—He's at work, and He's good at the details! You can relax into the protection of His providence right now by praying something like this:

the breaking and the remaking

God, I don't get it. I didn't plan for my life to turn out this way. But I know You're wiser than I am. I know You don't make mistakes. I choose to trust You.

I can't wait to see the story God writes for your life. Turn the page to read how He brought beauty out of ashes in my life through this major disappointment.

YOUR JOURNAL CORNER

In what way has your life turned out differently from what you expected? How has God used your greatest disappointment to make you more like Jesus (Romans 8:29)? How does God's providence comfort you?

beauty from ashes

While one dream was dying, God was resurrecting another long-buried dream.

You remember the day Jim invited me to visit him for a week? Well, the day before he called, Moody Publishers asked me to write a book. Seriously! They had been reading my blog posts for a while and liked what they saw.

So all that fall, I asked God what His assignment was for me:

Is it writing this book for Moody? Proceeding with Jim? Or something different entirely? Please make it so plain to me and give me the courage, humility, and grace to follow Your leading.

Why, God?

And then in early December—as you already know—my relationship with Jim came to an end. I felt the loss of his friendship deeply and questioned in my journal:

I trusted You, God—I finally trusted You. But You didn't allow it to proceed. Why?

I was still wrestling with that question more than a month later when I wrote:

I put my hand over my mouth, and I repent. I have been putting You on trial, God. This twenty-eight-year-old has been judging You, the eternal God, saying, "I don't think I needed another wound of this nature. I've already learned my lessons." I have found fault with You. Forgive me. Grant me acceptance and peace. You're wanting me to trust You even when I can't see what You're up to. If You did it, God, it is good. May that always be enough for me.

And then, in early March, I caught at least a glimpse of the answer I'd been searching for:

If things had moved forward with Jim, I'd only care about myself and my little dream coming true. But through this, God, you're making me a woman who "proclaims the excellencies of him who called me out of darkness into his marvelous light" (1 Peter 2:9).

If Jim and I had gotten together, I probably wouldn't have had the motivation to write this book. I would've been content to selfishly enjoy my little fairy tale.

The Ugly Subject of Beauty

Instead of living a fairy tale, though, I found myself wrestling with the ugly subject of beauty. When Jim confessed that "the spark came and went" for him, the Liar (Satan) attacked me once more with that big, hairy lie, "You're not beautiful." This lie rang in my ears for months until God used the tree outside my window to silence it.

One morning when I lifted the bathroom blinds, it nearly took my breath away—this delicate, purple flowering tree reaching up, up, up. While washing my face and combing my hair, I kept glancing at its beauty, drinking it in. That's when the tree's Creator impressed two things on me:

> *I make beautiful things.*

And,

> *You don't have to listen to Jim's voice.*

This tender expression of God's love was just what I needed. It not only soothed the lingering pain but reminded me, Oh, yeah! I don't have to believe every voice I hear. There is only one voice I can trust:

> The sheep hear [the Shepherd's] voice, and he calls his own sheep by name and leads them out. . . . The sheep follow him, for they know his voice. A stranger they will not follow, but they will flee from him, for they do not know the voice of strangers. (John 10:3–5)

That day, I decided to listen to the voice of the Maker of that beautiful, flowering tree outside my bathroom window. I began choosing to agree with the writer of Psalm 139:14:

> I praise you, for I am fearfully and wonderfully made.
>> Wonderful are your works;
>> my soul knows it very well.

God had used Jim's admission that he wasn't super attracted to me to help set me free from years of "beauty lies."

Let's Write This Thing!

And then I saw God answer my prayers to use the weakest area of my life to showcase His strength. I told Moody Publishers yes and began to write *Confessions of a Boy-Crazy Girl*, praying big prayers all the way:

> *Through this book, God, would You give girls a vision so far beyond just getting a guy? You can do anything. You can provide me and every girl out there with a husband, even if it seems humanly impossible. You can also do so much more. You could raise up an army of girls who know and trust You, understand and believe the gospel, and work hard to advance Your kingdom rather than wasting their lives dreaming of guys. Would You use this book to switch their focus?*

Making God Famous: Three Case Studies

God wants to do it in you too, you know. He wants to make Himself famous through your one little life, just like He's doing in my little life, and just like He did in the lives of a blind man and Lazarus. Watch how He works.

Case Study 1: A Blind Man

> As [Jesus] passed by, he saw a man blind from birth. And his disciples asked him, "Rabbi, who sinned, this man or his parents, that he was born blind?" Jesus answered, "It was not that this man sinned, or his parents, but that the works of God might be displayed in him." (John 9:1–3)

For years, this man never saw his mother's smile, whitecaps on a lake, or a golden sunset. He suffered blindness day after week after month in order to become a candidate for God's power to be displayed in his life. And, boy, was it ever on display the day Jesus covered his eyes with a mixture of saliva and dirt and told him to go wash—and he came back seeing!

Case Study 2: Jesus' Friend Lazarus

> A certain man was ill, Lazarus of Bethany.... So the sisters sent to [Jesus] saying, "Lord, he whom you love is ill." But when Jesus heard it he said, "This illness does not lead to death. It is for the glory of God, so that the Son of God may be glorified through it." (John 11:1, 3–4)

A couple of days later, though, Lazarus did die. So why did Jesus say the sickness wouldn't end in death? I think it's because He knew the end from the beginning. He knew that four short days later He would raise Lazarus from the dead, and many Jews would believe in Him as a result.

Interesting, isn't it? God decided ahead of time how these men would glorify Him—and it usually meant death. Either physical death or death of a dream.

Case Study 3: You

You (and I) aren't the exception. Life is still all about God, not us. And only the God who experienced death Himself could plan it this "backward" way:

> Unless a grain of wheat falls into the earth and dies, it remains alone; but if it dies, it bears much fruit. Whoever loves his life loses it, and whoever hates his life in this world will keep it for eternal life. (John 12:24–25)

So how about it, sweet girl? Will you forgo the fairy tale you long for in order to live for the God who lived and died for you? Will you die to your own small (but dear!) dreams in order to allow God to display His awesome power through your life?

You won't regret it.

And if you still have no idea how to stop living for guys and start living for God, let me share what a Scottish man and a diet taught me about giving the boot to my idols.

YOUR JOURNAL CORNER

Is it news to you that life is really all about
God and not about you? How can you
become a more God-focused girl rather
than a self-focused girl?
What is the weakest area of your life, and
how might God want to showcase His
strength in that area so others can see His
power on full display? (If you feel stuck,
ask your mom or someone who knows you
well to help you think through this.)

how it all ends

It took me just ten days after ending things with Jim to realize that in the future I would probably still be tempted to look to guys to satisfy me. I wrote:

> *God, I thought because You helped me so much with Jim I would never be the same again, that I would never be tempted in similar ways. I was wrong. If I'm not constantly being satisfied with Your love, my heart will be drawn right back to my idols. Protect me. I don't want to get into a relationship on the rebound. Oh, Jesus, would You be so near?*

Like I said, I'm still learning! Even now, when I interact with guys, my mind often jumps too far ahead into the future. I talked about that earlier—how I tend to search for clues that guy friends like me. My female brain connects dots that don't even exist, and I find myself light-years ahead of God—and therefore out of His peace.

Yep, the subtitle of this book is "On Her Journey from Neediness to Freedom" for a reason—it's a journey!

Idol Crushing

I'm not the only one tempted to turn back to my idols. Over and over in the Old Testament, God's people crushed their idols only to remake them and go right back to them.

Turns out, crushing idols and turning to God isn't a once-in-a-lifetime experience but a moment-by-moment journey. That's why, nearly every morning, I pray Psalm 90:14:

Satisfy [me] in the morning with your steadfast love,
that [I] may rejoice and be glad all [my] days.

Being satisfied with God's far better love is the only way boy-craziness won't consume my life and yours. And that's exactly what Thomas Chalmers and a diet taught me.

Thomas Chalmers was a pastor in nineteenth-century Scotland, and his sermon "The Expulsive Power of a New Affection" captured my heart immediately. The gist of it is that you can't talk yourself out of loving someone or something. Your emotions simply won't cooperate. But you can find someone or something even more lovely to delight in.

What My Diet Taught Me

I experienced this principle firsthand the month my doctor put me on a strict diet without sugar, bread, and lots of other yummy foods. It sounded like torture, pure and simple. I honestly didn't know how I'd survive. I was certain I'd spend the entire month dreaming about and drooling over iced sugar cookies, Nerds, and chocolate chip cookie dough ice cream.

But an astonishing thing happened. I didn't even miss my beloved sugar. You know why? Instead of snacking on raw broccoli all month (yuck!), I went to the health-food store, researched interesting recipes, and spent hours in the kitchen preparing unique dishes. Was it a lot of work? You'd better believe it. But was it even tastier than processed, refined sugar? Absolutely.

That, my friend, is how you get rid of an idol—by investing your time in relishing something (or Someone!) better. It's what Psalm 34:8 tells us to do:

> Taste and see that the Lord is good!
> Blessed is the man [and girl] who takes refuge in him!

As you pursue Christ with everything in you—as you put extra effort into tasting and seeing His goodness—you'll find that your "little g" gods don't appeal to you like they once did.

So, Is It Wrong to Ask God for a Guy?

Does that mean you should just ignore your strong desire for a guy and act like those feelings don't exist?

Not too long ago, I found myself asking a similar question: Is it sinful for me to keep asking God for a husband? After all, that door seemed to be sealed shut.

So I asked God to show me if it was okay. A few days later, while reading about the night of Jesus' arrest, I found my answer.

Taking Lessons from Jesus' Prayer

The night Jesus was arrested, we find Him in the olive groves of Gethsemane with three of His students—praying. Let's take a look:

> He . . . began to be greatly distressed and troubled. And he said to them, "My soul is very sorrowful, even to death."
> . . . Going a little farther, he fell on the ground and prayed that, if it were possible, the hour might pass from him. And he said, "Abba, Father, all things are possible for you. Remove this cup from me. Yet not what I will, but what you will." (Mark 14:33–36)

Really? Jesus prayed that He might not have to die? But He was God. He knew He had to face the cross—that's the whole reason He had come to earth! Still, Jesus was also fully man. And in His humanity, He asked God the Father for a way out.

In fact, in Matthew 26:44 we learn that Jesus prayed the same prayer three times in a row: "He went away and prayed for the third time, saying the same words again."

Jesus didn't let up. Three times He repeated the same request. That encourages me that I can ask, and ask, and ask God again for what I want.

"Nevertheless," Jesus always added, "not as I will, but as you will. Your will be done."

This shows me that I can keep asking as long as I don't demand my way but surrender to God's plan for my life. That's what Paul Miller points out in *A Praying Life*:

> Jesus neither suppresses his feelings nor lets them master him. . . . Desire and surrender are the perfect balance to praying.[14]

So I'm praying, asking boldly, for God to send an amazing husband my way in His perfect timing. And I'm recruiting others to pray with me.

How It All Ends

But what if He doesn't? What if God never grants my desire for a husband? No doubt about it, I'll have plenty more opportunities ahead for fresh, ongoing surrender. But regardless of His answer, I'll be okay. Actually, much, much more than just okay.

I love what a friend once told me. God has three answers to prayer: Yes, not yet, and I have something better. I trust Him to answer me in any of those three ways.

After all, did you know that marriage as we know it, between one man and one woman, is temporary? Luke 20:35 explains that there won't be marriage in heaven. Marriage is a faint picture for right now that points to something infinitely better: the love, oneness, and intimacy we will soon experience with Jesus.

The fact is, I will be married after this short life is over. Revelation 19:6–7 tells me so:

. . . Hallelujah!
For the Lord our God the Almighty reigns.
Let us rejoice and exult
and give him glory,
for the marriage of the Lamb has come,
and his Bride has made herself ready.

Who is this Lamb-groom? It's Jesus, who was sacrificed for your sins and mine. And this bride? That's you and me—if we're trusting in Jesus' righteousness on our behalf. We're part of the church He died for. And on this coming wedding day, Jesus will "present the church to himself in splendor, without spot or wrinkle or any such thing, that she might be holy and without blemish" (Ephesians 5:27).

That's why I'm okay with leaving my here-and-now story hanging with a big, fat question mark. My story is not finished. Your story is not finished.

And King Jesus' story is still being written, too. Soon He will return to set up His kingdom and marry His Bride (that's us!). And because our stories are wrapped up in His, regardless of the outcome here and now in the guy department, the best is most definitely yet to come.

YOUR JOURNAL CORNER

Are you demanding your desires, or are
you bringing them to your Father God?
Will you do so now in the space below?
What can you start to do today to pursue
Jesus with everything in you so that your
"little g" gods start to lose their appeal?

acknowledgments

Call me a nerd, but the first place I turn in a book is the acknowledgments page. So if you're reading this, I like you already. Now, where to begin? So many have helped and encouraged me along the way. But special thanks to:

Holly Kisly. When you first approached me, I wasn't clear if you were actually asking me to write a book or just wanting me to gather research for *someone else's* book, and it seemed too presumptuous to ask for clarification. Thanks for believing in me from the beginning and holding my hand through the process.

Dawn Leuschen. What a fearsome thing to trust someone with the first look at your words. I'll never forget Monday evenings at Union Coffee House, editing feverishly when our brains felt like mush after a long day at the office.

Dad and Mom, Kristie King, Hannah Lannigan, Kim Gwin, Brian Hedges, Jeff Norris, Brad Neese, Carrie Ward, Terri and Danielle Paulk, Katie DeRosa, Kristin Pool, Ginni Mathis, Laura Green, Janet Johnson, Sandra Hawkins, Susanna Totems, and *Sue Rhodes.* Thank you for reading the manuscript and providing excellent feedback. Your time, help, and encouragement were invaluable.

Lydia Brownback. I prayed you would be my official editor and was delighted when God said, "Yes." Thank you for all your hard work!

Nancy Leigh DeMoss. I can't thank you enough for stepping in at the eleventh hour and giving me the feedback I needed to make a good book a great book.

Mike Neises. I never would have made it past the contract stage if you hadn't cracked the code for this legal jargon-illiterate girl. Thank you!

Carla Shier. Thank you for sustaining me with yummy, healthy lunches while I was too busy writing to find my way into the kitchen.

Rene Hanebutt and the entire Moody Publishers team. Thanks for the numerous details you oversaw that I don't even know about to this day.

Wilson and Laura Green. Your peaceful home was the perfect place to write a book. Thank you for opening your home and lives to me these past three years.

Wes, Martin, Mike, and Nancy. Thank you for your support through this entire project, even when it meant less time writing for *Revive Our Hearts.* I can't imagine a better place to work, and that's because ROH is made up of leaders like you.

My prayer team. I am humbled by the many prayers you breathed over this project. Don't stop now!

Most of all, thank You, God. I never knew I could be so free, and I know this is just the beginning. I love You.

Please visit me at BoyCrazyGirlBook.com

notes

1. I learned the term "severe mercy" from Sheldon Vanauken, *A Severe Mercy: A Story of Faith, Tragedy, and Triumph* (New York: HarperOne, 1977), 211.

2. Nancy Leigh DeMoss, *Choosing Forgiveness: Your Journey to Freedom* (Chicago: Moody Publishers, 2006), 41.

3. Sally Lloyd-Jones, *The Jesus Storybook Bible: Every Story Whispers His Name* (Grand Rapids, MI: Zonderkidz, 2007), 36.

4. J. Oswald Sanders, *The Incomparable Christ* (Chicago: Moody Publishers, 2009), 86.

5. Ibid., 86–87.

6. This quote has been widely circulated and variously attributed.

7. "Acres of Hope" by Shane & Shane, 2004. Used by permission.

8. Randy Alcorn, *Ninety Days of God's Goodness: Daily Reflections That Shine Light on Personal Darkness* (Colorado Springs, CO: Multnomah, 2011), 21–22.

9. Ibid., 27.

10. Elisabeth Elliot, *The Path of Loneliness: Finding Your Way Through the Wilderness to God* (Ann Arbor, MI: Servant, 2001), 69.

11. Tullian Tchividjian, *Jesus + Nothing = Everything* (Wheaton, IL: Crossway, 2011).

12. William Cowper, "God Moves in a Mysterious Way," 1774.

13. Derek W. H. Thomas, *What Is Providence?* (Phillipsburg, NJ: P&R Publishing, 2008), 5.

14. Paul Miller, *A Praying Life: Connecting with God in a Distracting World* (Colorado Springs, CO: NavPress, 2009), 123.

A **true wŏman** BOOK

The goal of the **True Woman** publishing line is to encourage women to:

- *Discover, embrace, and delight in God's divine design and mission for their lives*
- *Reflect the beauty and heart of Jesus Christ to their world*
- *Intentionally pass the baton of Truth on to the next generation*
- *Pray earnestly for an outpouring of God's Spirit in their families, churches, nation, and world*

To learn more about the **True Woman movement** and the many resources available for individuals, small groups, and local church women's ministries, visit us online:

- *www.ReviveOurHearts.com*
- *www.TrueWoman.com*
- *www.LiesYoungWomenBelieve.com*

The **True Woman Manifesto** summarizes the core beliefs at the heart of this movement. You can sign the manifesto, find a downloadable PDF, and order additional copies at:

- *www.Truewoman.com/Manifesto*

True Woman is an outreach of:

Revive Our Hearts®

Calling women to freedom, fullness, and fruitfulness in Christ

P.O. Box 2000 | Niles, MI 49120

UNCOMPROMISING

978-0-8024-1167-9

Ask any girl on the street what womanhood is about, and you'll get a blank stare in return. No one knows. Young women are devoid of vision beyond popularity, material wealth, a cute boyfriend or a dream career. Even in Christian circles, significant questions are often left unanswered: What's the point of purity? Modesty? Femininity? What's biblical womanhood? Most of all, girls wonder at the longing in their souls for something greater. *Uncompromising: A Heart Claimed By a Radical Love* cuts straight to the heart of young womanhood.

Also available as an ebook

MOODY
PUBLISHERS

www.MoodyPublishers.com

AND THE BRIDE
WORE WHITE

978-0-8024-0813-6

Each chapter of *And the Bride Wore White* begins with a narrative of Dannah Gresh's young love life, taken from her own teenage journals. She transparently shares her struggles and successes, her moments of pain followed by healing and the moments of triumph. This story-line grips the young reader while they learn statistically proven risk-reduction factors. The end result are usable "how-to-say-no" skills that can reduce the risk of a young woman's heart being broken by sexual sin.

Also available as an ebook

MOODY
PUBLISHERS

www.MoodyPublishers.com